The Man in the Dog Park

The Man in the Dog Park

Coming Up Close to Homelessness

Cathy A. Small
With Jason Kordosky and Ross Moore

Cornell University Press

Ithaca and London

Permission to reprint the quotation from Thich Nhat Han from *The Heart of Understanding: Commentaries on the Prajnaparamita Heart Sutra (20th anniversary edition)*, Parallax Press, United Buddhist Church 2009, first published in 1988 that appears in chapter 2, has been granted by Parallax Press.

The authors express their deep thanks to Do Mi Stauber for her expert indexing of this book.

First published 2020 by Cornell University Press

Printed in the United States of America

Library of Congress Cataloging-in-Publication Data
Names: Small, Cathy, author. | Kordosky, Jason, author. | Moore,
   Ross (Homeless person), author.
Title: The man in the dog park : coming up close to homelessness /
   Cathy A. Small ; with Jason Kordosky and Ross Moore.
Description: Ithaca: Cornell University Press, 2020. | Includes
   bibliographical references and index.
Identifiers: LCCN 2019038321 (print) | LCCN 2019038322 (ebook) |
   ISBN 9781501748783 (hardcover) | ISBN 9781501748790 (epub) |
   ISBN 9781501748806 (pdf)
Subjects: LCSH: Homeless persons—United States. | Homelessness—
   United States.
Classification: LCC HV4505 .S64 2020 (print) | LCC HV4505 (ebook) |
   DDC 362.5/920973—dc23
LC record available at https://lccn.loc.gov/2019038321
LC ebook record available at https://lccn.loc.gov/2019038322

Contents

Preface

In Buddhist thought, compassion (*karuna*) is described as the quivering of the heart in relation to the suffering of others; it is accompanied by an impulse to relieve the suffering witnessed. Compassion is considered a natural human response, but it arises only when the walls of "otherness"—born of fear or disdain, greed or judgment—are not set in stone to block it.

This is why there is something to be said about the purposeful effort to step outside of your own reality. (Or is it actually to allow other realities, other lives, into your own?) When I have truly done this in my own life—moving into a village on a South Pacific island, taking a year off as a professor to live as a freshman in an undergraduate college dorm, or finding an authentic friendship with a homeless man—the results have been life-altering and, often, life-giving too. I think this is because such experiences upend our sense of what is true; they open us to the fine details of realms that others inhabit, stretching the boundaries of our insight and also our compassion.

This was not where I found myself more than a decade ago when I first met Ross Moore, a homeless man in a dog park. I am very aware and not very proud of how I first reacted, with profound distrust and fear. But I am just part of a culture. I would have to be a more remarkable person than I am to have acted otherwise.

More than ten years later, it is easier to see who he is and what I am, too, because the two are related. Every other world I have entered has offered me a window into my own, at the same time as it immersed me in other lives that came to touch me deeply enough to alter my perspectives, sometimes even my path.

I suppose this is why I, and Jason Kordosky, a coauthor, both became anthropologists, although our "anthropology" is as much a perspective of intimacy and nonjudgment as a profession. The fruits of this perspective have been profound and far-reaching for us both. Like others who cross cultures or the boundaries of our upbringing, we find in ourselves not only a greater responsiveness to the human condition but also the delight of living in a world less alien, less hostile, less unloving than it felt before.

The cover image invokes "the man in the dog park" whom I first saw as a homeless figure with a capital H and all the adjectives and sentiments, reactions and baggage, that come with that. So, let's begin there, with our own stereotypes. It is where I began too.

The Man in the Dog Park

1

The Beginning

It was 2008, we think. Ross doesn't remember the details of the very first time we met, but I do. I had entered the dog park early, as I do every morning with my three dogs. It must have been getting toward winter, because the park just before 7 am was not yet fully light, and I was aware of the man already seated on a bench inside the park. I had not seen him before. He was in his fifties, with a solid build and a very full, thick graying beard. His army green jacket seemed soiled, and he kept his eyes lowered as I entered. I looked quickly around to see that he had come with a dog, and indeed a mixed chow was sniffing in the distance within the enclosed, treed, block-long rectangle that serves as a municipal dog park. I felt a bit more at ease seeing the dog, but still, I remember making sure, in my old New York way, that I was always closer to the one entrance gate than this other figure in the park.

My fear and discomfort then embarrass me a decade later, now that Ross, the man in the park, has become a friend. It is not that my city radar was fully off-kilter. Ross lived in the woods with his dog; he was also a former felon. It's just that, like any of our labels, these do not really tell us much of true importance.

At the park, there were many more mornings when Ross and I observed each other before exchanging more than nods.

I remember noticing how well Ross cared for his dog, and how much his dog cared for him. Regulars at the dog park quickly become its citizens, sometimes its nosy neighbors. Who cleans up and who doesn't. Whose dogs are not controlled. Who fills the empty dog bowls with fresh water. Ross was just plain and simple a good citizen and, for me, even a hero. When, one morning, I became unwittingly embedded in a dogfight with five or more snarling, snipping dogs, it was Ross who came running to save me from an errant dog bite.

We exchanged first names, and then some superficial details of our lives, much later deeper words and addresses. Ross lived in the woods outside city limits, because sleeping inside the limits invited the police. He worked, on and off, at different jobs. He was, at points, a day laborer, taking sundry construction jobs. A trucking repair garage hired him after he performed well on a multiple day labor stint, but then the recession . . . and he was among the first to be laid off. At the time I had begun to know him better, he was working as a painter—hired onto a work crew for a multi-home project at the east end of town. When the project ended, so did his job. That was often how it went. Working and not working, with an occasional paycheck going toward a couple of nights at a motel, but mostly storing away some cash for food on the non-working days.

Ross told me that he was married, but his wife had a bed in her mother's home, some fifty miles away, because she could not abide life in the forest. After three years, having never met the elusive wife, "Wendi," I had my doubts. The process of friendship was not immediate for either of us.

Ross describes his early days at the park like this:

I came to [this town] looking for work and housing. I had little money and few prospects, a situation I have become accustomed to over the years. It was time to start again. I knew [this place] is blessed with a forest surrounding the city, which was ideal for camping out without being harassed by the police.

So here we are, my dog Cinders and I, working the labor pools during the day and living in the forest. We didn't know anyone, so it took me a month or two to find my way around town. Finding the "bark park" was a blessing for Cinders. Coming to work with me every day, she just had to sit there, but the park allowed a safe spot for her to run while I could relax a little. It soon became a routine for us, a stop in the morning before work and then again in the late afternoon before heading out into the forest.

The morning stop in particular allowed me to start meeting people. Some people talked to me more than others. And one of those people turned out to be Cathy. It took time, but our conversations got past "hi" and the weather. After I wrote this, Cathy asked me why I said "some people talked to me more than others" rather than "I talked— or liked to talk—to some people more than others." When I think about it, it's because being homeless, and sometimes seeming homeless in my appearance or manners, it's better to leave the approaching up to others. You know what I mean?

The longer I have known Ross, the more his integrity has impressed itself on me. In our conversations together, he shaded his history less than I did. He shared both his military service and his felony conviction; his childhood in Maryland along with his homelessness and his years in jail. The marriage turned out to be true, and when Ross was able to move out of the woods and into a subsidized room in a "welfare motel," Wendi moved back in with him. As I type this, tomorrow is Christmas Day, and Ross and Wendi are coming to dinner.

In the books that I write, I am always a learner more than an authority. What invites a book in my mind is my own process of learning. So it is with this book. I am a cultural anthropologist, but homelessness is not my area of knowledge or expertise. My career has had nothing at all to do with homeless issues or policy. This book was spurred by a chance encounter, a recognition of my own limitations and walls, a curiosity that melded with compassion over the years; it brought me to a profound awareness of a "life," individual and collective, that I had not sensed before. I thought it worth sharing.

Once it occurred to me that perhaps I was writing a book, after I jumped through the hoops of "human subjects" approval, after I formulated my questions for interviews, it also occurred to me that maybe it was better that *we* write a book. Ross and I. In a book that purports to offer a window into homelessness, why not a homeless author? His views of appropriate topics to include or perspectives to offer might well be different from a sympathetic outsider's view of what is important to know about being homeless. And as the project went on, another possibility presented itself. What if Ross could serve as an interviewer too, so the questions that elicited information also came from a differently informed perspective?

However intriguing the idea of a homeless co-authored book on homelessness, it would not have been workable without the personal qualities of Ross himself. Ross is a keen observer and, in many ways, a natural anthropologist. He has a curious ability to see events from multiple vantage points and extend his vision beyond his personal purview. After a police profiling event (see chapter 3), which I witnessed up close, I asked him about the frequency of such events in the lives of homeless people he knew. *"Of course, yeah, this happens a lot,"* he acknowledged, then added, *"but if they* [the police] *didn't do it, they couldn't do their jobs."* The gracious perspective surprised me, and he later expressed a similar magnanimity with regard to social workers, who, in many encounters, could seem bureaucratic, officious, and all about their paperwork. *"You've got to appreciate,"* he remarked, *"how overwhelmed they must feel, given their caseloads . . . I try to not keep calling them* [when he's trying to get an issue resolved] *because they get mad, and what else could you expect to happen?"*

The day at the dog park when I asked Ross whether he'd like to collaborate on writing a book on homelessness was in August 2013. His first response was *"You're crazier than I am!"* But he smiled as he said it and I could see he was pleased, too. The next day at the park he said he was on board, and within one week he had penned an outline of topics that he thought should be in the book on yellow lined paper. Ross never did get comfortable doing interviews himself, so his contribution is more about sharing his opinions, offering a sounding board for perceptions and insights, and providing the stories of his life.

The chapters that follow are not really about Ross, or our relationship—although incidents from Ross's life and our encounters pepper the chapters. It is about the experience of homelessness, seen often from a homeless point of view. I draw heavily on Ross's experiences, which he shares intimately, while the stories in the book also come from many other homeless folks who were interviewed by me and Jason Kordosky, a casino workers' union researcher who completed a master's degree in anthropology. Jason's research involved him in personal relationships and interviews with homeless day laborers, and he collaborated with me and Ross to structure this book. His perspectives, his interviews, his editing contributions, and his sensitivity to the issues were invaluable. Throughout the book, we also share direct descriptions of our own encounters, allowing readers to witness conversations and events they might not otherwise see. These are instructive not just as a window into the homeless perspective but as a way to shine a brighter light of awareness on our cultural perspectives and how we have come to view homelessness. It is a book that aims, then, to be about "us," too.

The details of homelessness that I glimpsed through my long-term relationship with Ross made me more aware of how my own perception of homelessness had been directed into the well-worn grooves of American narratives. Comb the newspapers and you will recognize them. There are the stories of homeless victim-hood: *Homeless Man Dies from Exposure*; *Homeless Woman Killed by Motorist*; *Homeless Inebriate Beaten in Park*. Just as familiar are headlines like this one—*"Boy Stabbed to Death after Giving a Homeless Man Money"*—that highlight homeless crime, mental illness, and addiction or public nuisance and deceit. (Aggressive panhandling; urinating in public; tent city eyesores; and rich, scamming beggars are but a few of the themes common here.) And then there are stories, usually around the holidays, captured in headlines like these this week in my local paper: *"Homeless Man Gets Help from Strangers,"* or *"Food Boxes for the Holidays Feed Hundreds of Homeless."*

Most Americans would find these a fair representation of homeless themes or headlines they have seen. It is not that these stories are untrue. It's simply that they represent a fragment of homeless life that fails to paint a portrait beyond a caricature. And really, to my anthropologist's eye, the portrait we see is sometimes more about the American public psyche than it is about homelessness. The chapters that follow offer a stark look at homelessness, but they offer an equally stark look at the gaze with which Americans (myself included) have come to frame what they see.

2

The Road to Homelessness

In the first year of Ross's and my formal collaboration, we would go on road trips together in our town, where I had lived for almost thirty years. It was always surprising, and often uncomfortable. "Pull over here," Ross would say, and we'd walk deep into the open field behind the gas station, and down a hill of undeveloped land that bordered nothing but power lines. In places like this, Ross would show me the sites where homeless people were living, or had lived. We'd uncover old panhandling signs or discarded bedding, or fresh garbage heaps in a drainage ditch that were signs of settlement. There was charred wood that had kept someone warm and pieces of cardboard that served as a mattress and backpacks visible in the drainage tunnels under the highway.

It was almost as if Ross had drawn me a new map of the town—of roads and ravines and highway underpasses and corners of the forest. His map included railway easements and other urban cavities where one could stay out of site; it showed the dirt lots and backstreets where vehicles that looked abandoned weren't really. Even the largest local shelter had entirely escaped my attention, tucked away in an industrial area where you'd have no occasion to go unless you worked there.

There were so many sites, so many people living this way. What causes a person to become homeless? It was a question that dominated my early interviews. It is also the question most asked by friends and acquaintances when they discover I have interviewed homeless people. Let me say that I have come to question the question. It sounds like a neutral inquiry, but consider the common cultural assumption behind the question, namely, that something about the person—an individual trait or condition—is at the root of his or her homelessness. We want there to be a reason, a personal cause. When we know the cause, we can then address the problem. The person is a perpetual drug or alcohol abuser; he got sick and didn't have insurance; she was laid off and had no job prospects because she dropped out of high school; he took out a mortgage he couldn't afford and lost his home to foreclosure; she argued with family to the point of a fissure and left home; he is a felon and can't get a job.

Sociologists call this an individual deviancy hypothesis. It is rooted, they argue, in political and economic ideologies that posit an equal and fair playing field, where people who do not make it to first base in the great game of life will be found to have personal flaws and a history of poor choices. Conversely, everyone standing on third base thinks they hit a triple, never questioning whether perhaps this was the base on which they were born.

As an anthropologist, I believe this concept of bounded, separate agent-selves that have the power to bring on their own destinies is an even more encompassing ideology, extending in our culture not just to economic success and failure but to whether you get cancer or survive an illness, whether you can win friends and influence people, and even whether or not you invite good luck. There is a reason why self-help books have been the fastest-growing segment of book sales among adults in the United States; it is our abiding

American belief in a self-made man/person in which the locus of power, fate, and fortune is largely internal.

Not all cultural traditions view things in this way. If you are having trouble seeing an alternative to the American/Western conception of things (the classic problem of a fish trying to see water), consider the way Thich Nhat Hanh, a Vietnamese Buddhist monk and activist, looks at a piece of paper. "There is a cloud," he writes, "floating in this sheet of paper." He continues:

> Without a cloud, there will be no rain; without rain, the trees cannot grow; and without trees, we cannot make paper. The cloud is essential for the paper to exist. If the cloud is not here, the sheet of paper cannot be here either. So we can say that the cloud and the paper inter-are . . .
>
> If we look into this sheet of paper even more deeply, we can see the sunshine in it. If the sunshine is not there, the forest cannot grow . . . And so, we know that the sunshine is also in this sheet of paper. The paper and the sunshine inter-are. And if we continue to look, we can see the logger who cut the tree and brought it to the mill to be transformed into paper. And we see the wheat. We know the logger cannot exist without his daily bread, and therefore the wheat that became his bread is also in this sheet of paper. And the logger's father and mother are in it too. When we look in this way, we see that without all of these things, this sheet of paper cannot exist.
>
> Looking even more deeply, we can see we are in it too. This is not difficult to see, because when we look at a sheet of paper, the sheet of paper is part of our perception.

Thich Nhat Han's concept of "interbeing" invites a different way of viewing both a piece of paper and a social problem. Each arises from a plethora of intersecting factors in which we all are ultimately implicated and playing a part.

Consider some of the intersecting factors at work in these four composite portraits, each representing some all too familiar statistics on the road to homelessness.

Portraits of Homelessness

Story 1

Like 15.5 percent of the U.S. population, "Yvonne" was born poor, and remained persistently so during her childhood. Although she was bright and finished high school, she was not one of the rare 3.2 percent of "persistently poor" who earn a bachelor's degree. With only a high school diploma, her job prospects were limited. She found steady but minimum wage work in the mailroom of a company on the bus route from her neighborhood and earned benefits and small but regular raises. This made rent affordable, so she and her longtime boyfriend lived together in one side of a duplex inhabited, on the other side, by its owner. A year after the U.S. recession began in 2007, though, Yvonne's boyfriend was laid off, straining their resources. Three months later, she was laid off as well. Their landlord, who had known both tenants for many years, allowed them to stay in the house until they got re-employed. Then the next shoe dropped.

The CNN Money headline in January 2009 read "Foreclosures Up a Record 81%," reporting a spike of more than 3.1 million foreclosure filings issued during 2008, or one of every fifty-four households. Amid the crisis brought on by predatory lenders operating with few government constraints, Yvonne's landlord was one of those who lost his

---

property. Yvonne became homeless, part of the 61 percent rise in homelessness that followed the recession, and she and her boyfriend became shelter residents. Approximately 40 percent of families who faced eviction due to foreclosure during this time were renters like Yvonne and her boyfriend.

Story 2

"Derrick" was legally considered an adult at eighteen in 2006, when he was caught with a stash of marijuana and drug paraphernalia. By 2006, what had changed most since the advent of the War on Drugs was the prosecution rate for crimes of possession, which had nearly tripled since 1982; 82.5 percent of drug-related arrests in this year were for possession only.

And Derrick is black. In 2006, African Americans accounted for 35 percent of all drug arrests, three times their proportion in the general population, despite similar reported drug use among all racial groups. Once a user has been arrested, the picture becomes statistically even more bleak. With mandatory sentencing laws, and more aggressive prosecution of users, approximately 93 percent of drug defendants adjudicated during 2006 were convicted, compared to 76 percent in 1981. Without the resources to hire a good private lawyer, Derrick was convicted of a felony, which placed him among the 33 percent of African American men who are or once were convicted felons. (The national rate of the "ever" felon population is 8 percent.)

He also went to jail. In state court in 2006, where we locate Derrick's case, 63 percent of defendants receiving felony convictions for drug possession were sentenced to prison or jail, while 37 percent—often those with strong legal representation—received probation or community service.

Although Derrick served only six months in a regional jail, the need to indicate his felony conviction on work applications meant that his many job applications were unsuccessful. As is true for two-thirds of newly released inmates, a supportive family helped Derrick stay on his feet while he looked for work, but there were few jobs available in his immediate community. Determined, Derrick broadened his job search to other cities and finally found work in another town as a service station attendant and apprentice mechanic.

Away from friends and relatives, he managed to rent an apartment with his wages and successfully restarted his life with a steady job at the service station. Six months into his employment, however, after a minor argument with his boss over a day off, he received two weeks' notice—a punitive pattern of employer conduct reported by many former inmates. Unable to find another job quickly enough to keep up with his rent, he was evicted from his apartment three months later. Like Derrick, 76 percent of former inmates reported that finding work after being released was "difficult or nearly impossible."

Now almost thirty, Derrick struggles as do most former felons to gain employment, often finding the only work available is day labor. Men with criminal records account for about 34 percent of all nonworking men aged twenty-five to fifty-four. Derrick moves in and out of homelessness, depending on work, with multiple addresses in a single year that flip between rooming houses, motels, and shelters.

The majority (67 percent) of surveyed male former felons were unemployed or underemployed five years after being released from prison.

Story 3

"Robert," was raised in a poor farming community in Georgia, named the "most patriotic state" because it contributes the largest population proportion of military recruits. He enlisted in the army after high school, deploying to Afghanistan. Robert began experiencing severe depression after he was honorably discharged from the military in his twenties. Diagnosed with PTSD, he had frequent episodes of fear and depression when he self-medicated with antidepressants and alcohol. Eight months after applying for disability compensation from the Veterans Administration, Robert was granted a 10 percent disability payment, the most common award, amounting to $127 per month in 2012.

Robert worked on and off, often losing his job when a flare-up of his illness resulted in unexplained absences. His wages, even when work was steady, together with his disability payment barely covered the cost of his rent; his apartment rental applications, after credit checks, were consistently denied. He would sleep on a friend's couch for a while, contributing what he could, until the friend's hospitality or the friendship was exhausted, only to find another friend's couch for another little while. This pattern of residence, called "couch surfing" by homeless or "doubling up" by social workers, is the most common prior living situation before becoming homeless.

The odds of homelessness multiply when temporary residence is complicated by drug or alcohol abuse and mental instability. Robert's situation is more the rule than the exception. A veterans' advocacy organization estimates that "half of homeless veterans suffer from mental illness; two-thirds suffer from substance abuse problems; and many from dual diagnosis," which is defined as a person struggling with both mental illness and a substance abuse problem. Military service pulls men and women away from their communities and families for long periods of time, often attenuating ties, and many return with a psychological or addiction problem that becomes too difficult for friends or families to handle. As social networks retreat, the probability of homelessness looms larger.

The veterans who ultimately end up homeless are but a small slice of the total veteran population, but they share two characteristics with Robert: they often have a significant disability; and they are also poorer than other veterans, sometimes as a result of their disability, but sometimes simply as a result of having fewer resources and having had fewer opportunities growing up. It is a startling fact that military pay grade, as a proxy for socioeconomic status, is a stronger predictor of veteran homelessness than even PTSD. Taken together, these factors all but seal Robert's fate.

In Arizona, where we interviewed, one in every six homeless people was a veteran during the time when Robert, after a year and a half of couch surfing, would become officially homeless. Robert would end up living unsheltered on the streets or in the woods, as do most homeless veterans, many balking at the sometimes onerous rules and restrictions of shelter life—as you will see in chapter 4.

Story 4

"Evelyn" followed her husband to a different state where he had family and had moved for a job. His was a modest but middle-class salary; her lesser-paid but full-time work as a clerk supplemented their income, allowing them to rent a nice apartment in a suburb near her husband's relatives. The abuse began shortly after the move, first verbal, then turning physical, and Evelyn found herself frightened and without any family network of her own to turn to. It went on for years. Whenever she would threaten to leave, he first would be contrite but then would become more abusive and menacing, warning her that she would live with him or not at all. Fearing for her safety, she finally summoned the courage to leave. She left her home and her work without notice or forwarding information, to protect herself against her husband.

Seven years after her marriage, Evelyn found herself in a strange city, with no income, no job, and no family. For women, domestic violence is a leading cause of homelessness. Like many women who must suddenly and clandestinely leave home, Evelyn discovered her only safe option to be a women's shelter. Supported by this transitional-only housing, she was able to find work in her new city, but after months of searching, she never located a permanent apartment that fit her budget. Evelyn found herself in the same boat as Robert (in story 3) and like a growing number of working poor: unable to afford spiraling rental prices, even with her forty-hour-weekly take-home pay.

The crisis in affordable housing has been growing each year since 2007. By 2012, more than 25 percent of renters were paying over 50 percent of their income in rent, a situation now termed "cost (or rent) burdened." Full-time work can no longer pay for a livable rental in many areas of the country, as rent price increases continue to outpace inflation. "In 2017 more than 70% of renters with annual incomes less than $15,000 and 25% of black households—compared with 13% of white households—spend more than half their incomes in rent," according to Harvard's Joint Center for Housing.

The National Low Income Housing Coalition provides a map and a tool called "Out of Reach," which lets you look up the hourly wage needed in your state to afford a modest apartment. In many states, including Washington, California, most of the Northeast, Colorado, Florida, Illinois, and Virginia, you need to make $20 per hour or more to afford an apartment. In my home state of Arizona, the needs are more moderate, and the housing cost rank is solidly in the middle, twenty-fifth in the nation. Even here, however, a salary of $17.56 per hour is needed to pay for a modest rental, which means that, at minimum wage, one must work seventy hours a week.

Evelyn simply gave up. Despite working full-time, she could not afford a decent apartment. The rooms she could afford were always in an area of town in which she felt unsafe. She moved into a public shelter and lists this as her address. In a 2014 survey of twenty-five U.S. cities, 15 percent of all homeless adults were, like Evelyn, identified as survivors of domestic violence.

So What "Causes" Homelessness?

It is not easy to parse out the specific interaction of personal, social, and structural factors that brings anyone's life to homelessness. In these stories one sees contributing individual circumstances and personal decisions, but there is also poverty, rent inflation, educational inequity, a low minimum wage, racism, predatory lending, domestic abuse, an unaddressed national drug problem, and an uneven legal system.

We might also have added a story about a fifteen-year-old girl, still homeless now in her late teens, who left or was forced to leave her home because she was gay. Homophobia is a leading cause of homelessness among U.S. youth. Medical problems and costs, another recurring theme in our interviews, often gut individual resources at the same time that they rob people of their ability to work, leaving many homeless. According to the U.S. Department of Housing and Urban Development, a significant number of homeless living in shelters are disabled—more than twice the percentage in the general population.

Beyond the multiple factors seen openly in the narratives are underpinnings, more deeply embedded in American life. As Daniel Weinberger identified more than two decades ago, these include structural changes in the U.S. economy that shipped factory jobs overseas (contributing, we would add, to growing U.S. wealth differentials); transformations in the national housing market; the lack of relative expansion in the government "safety net"; and, significantly, the pervasiveness of sociopolitical norms and attitudes that stigmatize the homeless in the policy sphere. We have continued decades later, as Judith Treas has pointed out, to maintain a view of homelessness that "blames the victim," vastly affecting how social policy is crafted.

So, is it the overarching structures, policies, and attitudes in American life that produce homelessness? Well, yes, all these factors set up critical conditions, but the answer is not exactly this either. For Thich Nhat Han, the sun doesn't *cause* the tree, although it is a necessary condition. All these factors construct the social and economic landscape that individuals must negotiate, and it is a geography of slippery slopes.

Despite the immense complexity here, it's simple, really. Every time the slopes are made steeper and more slippery still by larger conditions, more individuals slide into homelessness. Those with personal issues and challenges may slide first, but the slope can become too steep for almost anyone, however motivated or talented, to maintain his or her footing. And without a lifeline in the form of a network of family and friends with resources or available and adequate government programs, the chances are that a person will slip to a homeless bottom.

The general population has a one-in-two-hundred chance of ever becoming homeless—not a terribly steep slope. If you are born poor, the slope steepens almost eightfold. Hispanic or black? The odds of being born poor are more than double those of non-Hispanic whites. The probability that you will ever move out of poverty has actually decreased since the beginning of this century, and your chances of becoming homeless if you are born into poverty are only one in twenty-five. If you were in foster care, then your chances are one in six. Now add an economic downturn, and there is another precipitous drop. One in five people became jobless in the five years including and following the recession that began in 2007. Would you have been that one who lost his job? If you had only a high school diploma, your chances of being laid off were three times greater than a college graduate's. So what are your chances of being a college graduate? As with Yvonne in the first story, they are tiny if you were "persistently poor" growing up. Add to this any personal or social liability like an abusive husband or an alcohol problem or a depression disorder, and a plummet into homelessness becomes practically inevitable.

This is what we saw when we interviewed homeless people: a series of falls from successive slopes, set up by larger conditions, abetted by some personal decision or circumstance; each slip to a lower slope leads the person closer and closer to the edge until one single or small event triggers a seemingly sudden drop into homelessness.

It is telling that many homeless people understand their homelessness in the narrow terms of an individual event or trait, naming the precipitating push as the reason they are homeless. Here, paraphrased, are the reasons that homeless people we interviewed gave for their homelessness when asked directly why they were homeless:

> *My mother died, and I used all my money for her funeral.*
> *I had an accident and suddenly couldn't work or pay my rent.*
> *I owned a house that burned down and I didn't have insurance.*
> *My landlord (who had offered a very low rent I could afford) died.*
> *I moved for a job, but when I got there, I found it had already been filled.*
> *I had an argument with my boss over vacation and quit my job.*
> *After I got out of jail, my relatives didn't want me to live at home because of my crime.*
> *My roommate kept bringing strangers into the house . . . so I left.*

What is so striking about these answers is that they share with the American public a view that a minor flaw of fate or character produced their plight. In longer interviews, in which we had a chance to engage people more intimately, it was clear that a number of individuals understand their homelessness more fully, but they have learned to frame it in terms that they think a non-homeless public would understand. Still, many do not perceive their homelessness in wider terms and internalize the view that their homelessness is largely due just to "them" and their bad choices or bad luck.

Anyone who listens to these stories over and over is left with two seemingly contradictory facts. First, in most cases, homelessness would not have occurred without some particular personal action or mishap. Second, the probability that someone will become homeless is not really attributable to individual actions or events. Kim Hopper, a medical anthropologist who researches homelessness and advocates for homeless issues, has explained concisely how these two ideas can coexist. Individual-based factors convert to homelessness only under certain conditions.

In a very tangible sense, individual actions and their consequences are conditioned by the larger geography of the slopes on which those individuals are standing. Domestic abuse, drug or alcohol addiction, and mental illnesses all occur in a substantial portion of the general population, but it is clear that, in most cases, they do not cause those affected to become homeless. As one can see from the four stories told in this chapter, an individual's battle with depression or drugs or abuse results in homelessness only when certain other, usually larger conditions are present.

Our collective structures and policies are crucial drivers in amplifying the effects of individual decisions. Making a choice to smoke a joint, for instance, can have lifelong consequences if you are black, poor, and also living in the wrong neighborhood. On a slope already made slippery by a felony conviction and a weak education, then a fight with a boss, or too many sick days, a sudden accident, or a problem with alcohol, can then trigger a descent into homelessness.

What this means in a lived rather than just an analytic sense is that a person often has a gut feeling of continually skating on thin ice or walking on a precipice. Your footing can never be sure; and one tiny slip can send you underwater or over the edge. We have used the metaphor of slippery slopes in this chapter because it seems to capture these interlocking feelings of imbalance, dread, uncertainty, insecurity, and lack of control that we hear in the words of homeless people who try to describe to us their situation.

When Cal expressed to me the feelings he had about being homeless, his face noticeably contorted. His words came haltingly:

"It's a feeling in the pit of your stomach. A feeling of—of—what's taken away.

"Like a war. Waiting for the inevitable to happen."

Cal currently lives in subsidized housing. Although he is no longer officially homeless, he blames his years of living in shelters for a sense of imbalance or uncertainty that never leaves him.

That sense of imbalance was evident as well for Jerald, when he described the very first time he stayed in a shelter:

> When I finally realized that I was actually homeless, it was really unnerving and it forced me to adapt to a lot of different things that I wasn't really used to . . . Being somewhere where I knew I always had a place to go or a place to stay, a roof over my head, I could fall back on family to help me and everything. But being here . . .

His words attune the listener to his sense of dislocation, of living each day without a safety net to depend on.

Ross describes his feeling to me as *"always waiting for the other shoe to drop."* Even after he found housing, I noticed that he would stockpile cans of food. When I asked him about this, he responded thoughtfully, *"I know, I'm like that now. I'm always worried I'm not going to have enough food. So, I just stack cans so I know it's there."* Ross

continued reflecting, *"I don't know what it is about me. It's like . . .
Everything that can go wrong will go wrong."*

A feeling of being off balance . . . of not being able to count on
things . . . of tentative footing. This lived experience of walking
on a slippery slope is a recurring aspect of being homeless, but
just as in our composite sketches, for many individuals it is a nag-
ging feature of the road to homelessness as well. In the ten years
before Ross and his girlfriend, now wife, became more permanently homeless, they had fifteen different addresses. Sometimes
evicted, sometimes moving for a more promising job or cheaper
rent, they would drift in and out of homelessness as job layoffs
and loss dictated. Many pre-homeless and homeless individuals
inhabit this world of largely unauthored change that leaves them
in a constant state of uncertainty and upheaval. It has become
easier for me to see how the unrelenting instability month after
month, year after year, invites a state of fear, unease, and paranoia
that one often associates with being a cause of homelessness. In
how many Americans' minds is some sort of mental instability the
reason for a person's homelessness?

Kim Hopper, both researcher and homeless advocate, has
been tireless in his critique of the connection between mental
illness and homelessness seen in public and policy discourse.
He admonishes us to look at mental illness as perhaps a product of homelessness or a strategy for dealing with its conditions rather than a cause. The importance of his words goes
beyond letting us see more accurately the mutual causation
at work; it also lies in correcting a narrative that distances the
homeless from us as "other" and relegates them to a category
for which we feel pity but not empathy, to the point where the
sight of a homeless person causes us to cross the street rather
than lend a hand.

The public diagnosis of homelessness as a result of mental illness also feeds a narrative of separateness in research and policy. The homeless become a group apart, who cannot be understood in the same way that we might understand a relative or a friend. Public policy has long emphasized finding "them" a separate space, such as a shelter or tent city, rather than integrating homeless people into established neighborhoods with housing vouchers. Researchers study homelessness as if it were a subculture, separate from the mainstream, to be understood in its own right rather than, as Martha Burt has argued, reconfiguring our studies to see it as a part and product of the larger system. The result is an American viewpoint that wrests homelessness from its larger cultural fabric, rendering it and its inhabitants an aberration rather than an outgrowth of our system.

This separateness—this sense of being aberrant—was the part of homelessness that Cal, who uses meds to contain his depression, found most difficult. What most bothered him was, as Cal put it, being on *"the fringes of society."* The problem, he explained, was that *"I know what [normal society] is like, but I'm marginalized, not considered part of it anymore."*

What it feels like to be alien, what life becomes as "homeless," is the subject of the next chapter.

3

The Stigma of Being Homeless

As demanding and unpleasant as the physical conditions of being homeless are, they are not, for many, the primary challenge of being without a residence. One of the most difficult transitions for individuals in becoming homeless is taking on the homeless identity. As Greg told me:

> I was traveling through town, and camping where I could, hanging out in the park during the day, and someone in the park asks me, "Are you homeless?" and it surprised me. Even though I had been here a couple of months, I didn't think that way. I was just thinking I was traveling—you know, not settled yet. But when that question came—wow—I guess that's what I am now.

Think for a moment of what you would write—honestly—if you were asked to list in one minute as many adjectives as you could think of to describe a homeless person, someone in your mind's eye you had actually encountered. I invited a few hundred university students to do just this, and randomly selected one hundred of their one-minute jottings—"freelists" as they are called— to analyze. Although the freelists returned more than two hundred different descriptors, even after they were edited for synonyms, the picture they offered of the homeless was largely consistent and

FIGURE 3.1
Most frequent responses given by college students when asked for adjectives to describe a homeless person.

followed a pattern. In this "word cloud," you can see the responses that occurred the most frequently, the larger the text, the greater the frequency.

A few things stand out about the freelists, taken together. First is that the portrait is largely negative. Seventy-two percent of the sample had *only* pejorative adjectives to apply to the homeless, ranging in flavor from Pitiable and Alone to Dangerous and Deranged. The main category of negative representation could be called "aversion," in which words such as Smelly, Dirty, Disgusting, Unkempt, and Gross were common. But the negative words clustered as well around two other overlapping themes: irresponsibility and cluelessness (Drunk, Out of It, Confused, Lazy, Uncoordinated, Slow, Disorganized, Unaware) and a darker portrayal of the homeless as dangerous or deceptive (Aggressive, Annoying,

Scary, Terrifying, Mentally Ill, Compulsive, Loud, Mean, Pushy, Resentful, Ungrateful).

Yet even among the three-quarters of the sample who labeled homeless with adjectives that no one would want applied to themselves, there were frequent expressions of concern and pity. Homeless people were identified as Unloved (not unlovable), Needy, Helpless, and Lonely. They were rendered as Poor, Cold, Old, Hungry, Frail, Sick. It was unusual, even among the negative-only freelisters, to omit words of concern or pity. Only one in eight of these responders had no such words to offer, mentioning only the aversive or dangerous dimensions of homeless individuals.

A little more than a quarter of the sample group were able to go beyond expressions of pity and assign what might be termed "positive" attributes to the homeless, including multiple lists with the words Nice, Humble, Understanding, Survivor, Sincere, Respectful, Friendly, and Hopeful. Still, only one of the one hundred responders used solely positive descriptors. All of the other positive listers in the sample included both negative and positive terms in their lists, describing a homeless person, for instance, as Filthy or Drunk but also Kind.

These adjectives might fit into Teresa Gowan's useful framework for understanding American cultural narratives about homelessness. She identifies three discourses that people use to discuss and interpret homelessness: (1) sin-talk—touching on cloud words such as Aggressive, Lazy and Mean—in which homelessness is seen to arise from the character flaws or immorality of the homeless individual (this shows up in the sample more clearly, though less frequently, in words that did not make it into the word cloud, such as "criminal," "hustler," "freeloader," and "lowlife"); (2) sick-talk—invoking cloud words like Helpless, Frail, Needy, Out of It, "Mentally Ill—in which homelessness is framed as an illness that should be treated and cured; and (3) system-talk, in which homelessness is framed as the product of systemic injustice or instability with nouns such as Victim and Survivor in the word cloud. For Gowan, these narratives don't simply represent public perception; they enter, regionally and historically, into policy decisions. Indeed, they affect the homeless' view of themselves.

Being a "Homeless" Person

No one is more aware of the perceptions surrounding homelessness than the homeless themselves. In *At Home on the Street*, Jason Wasserman and Jeffrey Clair describe homelessness as a "master status," that is, a label that dominates all other forms of identity, overriding any other characteristic one might have. There is a point in all homeless people's lives when they first attach the label to themselves. When I interviewed homeless individuals, this turning point was one of the narratives they pursued. It was as if, only by situating in time the moment when the mantle of homelessness first fell on their shoulders, could individuals portray themselves in a life before becoming homeless; in this way, they separate their real selves from the stigmatized homeless label with which they were now tagged.

Malcolm, a shelter resident, described his homeless identity this way to Jason: *"Ever since I came in [to the shelter], automatically I just thought, 'Well, all right, I'm just going to be with a bunch of homeless guys, bunch of guys that pretty much don't know what they are doing' . . . I just had like a negative, like a little negative feeling about it."*

This "little negative feeling" was expressed to different degrees by many interviewees, and homeless individuals we met took pains not to fit the perceived stereotype. It is a form of "distancing," as it has been termed by David Snow and Leon Anderson, just one strategy for preserving a sense of self-worth by seeing who is homeless as "not me." For some, the goal was explicitly to "look normal." For most, who could not avoid appearing homeless, it was deliberately not fitting some prominent aspect of the label.

It was having combed hair and clean clothes. For Arthur, who did day labor construction work during the day and lived in a shelter, it was having his "clean pair" of clothes to wear out if he was walking in the street so he didn't appear so unequivocally homeless. For Hank, it was not having to sit noticeably without food or a lunch bag, as if he needed a handout, when the other men on the construction crew took their lunchtime break. Adam, and other shelter residents too, told Jason that they often left their backpacks at the shelter before walking outside, noting that an overstuffed backpack could be a "tell" that they were homeless. Oliver, another day laborer living at the local shelter, didn't want to appear drunk, a concern that he developed after a friend called him out on his appearance. He told Jason:

> Like one of my friends, he works, and I ran into him at [the shelter].
> He looks at me and he says, "Bro, you look like you've been drinking."
> I go, "What do you mean?"
> "'Cause your clothes are all dirty. I've never seen you like that."
> I said, "Hey, I worked today and I gotta do laundry and stuff so . . ."
> He goes, "Well that's good you're working but . . ."

Oliver took the message to heart, explaining his new strategy for looking clean in public: "That's why I wear the same clothes all week [at work]. My other clothes are clean so . . . I can just change out . . . So, I think ahead of time, you know."

Miriam was very conscious of smells. At the night shelter where she slept, when boxes and baskets of bedding would be carried in, Miriam would go through the boxes, sniffing each blanket or bedroll, putting back some and selecting others. When I asked her why she did that, she told me, *"I always smell the blankets . . . [If a blanket doesn't smell clean] you don't want to lay on that. Because that's going to get into your pores."*

Miriam, who had worked on and off as a night reception clerk, complained that it was hard to keep her body and clothes clean sometimes when she was living in shelters: *"I'll be trying to look for a job with my dirty clothes on. So that's kinda hard because they can tell."*

"So what do you do?" I asked her.

"What do you do?" she repeated back. *"I just rub soap on my clothes so they don't smell. Right now* [she glances at me with an embarrassed look] *I'm still wearing my clothes that I slept in last night. I just went into the bathroom and rubbed soap on them so they don't smell."*

For Ross, the aspect of the homeless persona that was most important to defy was an appearance of aggressiveness. As a bearded adult male typically dressed in a worn military jacket, he was aware that someone else's interpretation of him as threatening could easily lead to troubles of his own. His cardinal rule, which he applied to me when we first met, is *"Let people approach you."* Although Ross can be animated and talkative once you know him, his initial persona seems passive and reserved, almost taciturn.

Subverting the homeless stereotype is sometimes a matter of honor, but sometimes, too, it is a matter of successfully avoiding consequential encounters. One day Ross and I were at the dog park. He was seated at a picnic table; I was standing. We had a lively conversation going as a black-and-white patrol car pulled into the macadam parking lot adjacent to the dog park. I noticed the car make a right turn from the road into the lot and figured the police would drive by, seeing no commotion or dogfights, and exit the other side. But the car stopped, and a fortyish uniformed white patrol officer emerged from the vehicle. I looked to see what he was attending to as he walked toward the dog park gate.

The officer came through the gate and straight over to us, turning his head pointedly toward Ross: *"You live in the neighborhood?"*

"Good morning, officer," I heard Ross respond, and then I lost track, scouring my own arsenal of middle-class capital for the right things to say. Clearly more nervous than Ross, I awkwardly inserted little uninvited comments into their conversation. *"Yeah, you know, Ross and I have been regulars at this park for years now."* The officer glanced in my direction, returning his gaze to Ross, never once speaking to me. *"Hey, Ross,"* I bumbled, *"remember the time back when we first met when we . . . ?"* Ross smiled a bit and nodded. The specifics of what I related escape me now, but I vividly recall my panicked intent to establish that I knew him well and that his residence in town went back years. (At the time, he was sleeping—illegally—in the woods.)

The officer's interview lasted only a few minutes. *"You have a good day,"* he said as he turned to leave the park, but the message was unmistakably "I've decided not to pursue this." The officer had been respectful and professional, but I felt a little shaken by the encounter. *"He profiled you,"* I said to Ross. *"Doesn't that bother you?"*

"What do you expect?" was Ross's retort. *"The police can't do their job if they can't approach people who don't look right to them."* It's a toughly gracious act of acceptance, I thought to myself, when the person who doesn't look right is you.

The consciousness of being and looking "not right" is a regular companion of homeless people, even when it is sometimes just an internal sense. I would not have known that Kevin, who solicited money at a shopping center exit with a "HUNGRY, HOMELESS,

HANDICAPPED" sign, was homeless were it not for his panhandling. He would sit in a folding chair, grandfatherly in his sixties, with a collared oxford shirt, a wool winter coat, and polished shoes. Still, he consistently talked about himself in our conversations as *"a street bum like me."*

"Why do you say that?" I asked him once, feeling the sting of that description. *"Because that is what I am"* was his response.

Home-Free and Houseless

Not all homeless wear the homeless label without resistance. Jason interviewed a number of day laborers, many of whom were young men, living in local shelters or on the street. *"Are you homeless?"* he would ask. *"No, I'm home-free,"* was sometimes the reply. The term was used with him both tongue-in-cheek, in the shelter, and less jokingly, on the street, where Jason saw it as a way to resist the stigma of homelessness. In this sense it aligns with national developments among some homeless and homeless advocates who have moved to the term "houseless." Here's how the "houseless" state the plight of stigma on the website, houseless.org:

> Those who are forced into being without an abode and/or dwelling are all too quickly deemed less than citizens. In many regards are even treated as less than human. How about thinking that we are NOT homeless, nor last-class citizens or non-human? We think, have feelings, have intellect and struggle. How would you feel to be thought of as anything less than human just for circumstances due to those of profit/gain/control?

The monikers "houseless" and "home-free" are meant to evade the cluster of social meanings attached to being homeless. Yet whether or not shelter and street dwellers construct a different frame of self-reference, the public does not always cooperate in the re-signification. The "carefree," "unfettered," or "independent" quality of houseless life that home-free advocates wish to convey is not totally absent from wordlists in my sample. Nevertheless, they constitute a tiny category of description (about 1 percent) that would not likely make it into the world cloud of frequently used terms among any sample of Americans. Instead, the major descriptive themes that went beyond the nefarious or worthless cast the homeless as passive victims, far from the vision of "intellect and struggle" that the website of the houseless aims to advance.

Media coverage of the homeless does little to invite an alternative vision. News headlines about the homeless often reiterate the themes captured in the freelists—homeless victimhood, homeless survivorship, homeless nuisance or aversion, homeless aggression and deception—and rarely does a reporter include multiple perspectives in the same article. With this steady perceptual diet, a consuming public is tugged between polar inclinations of pity and fear, compassion and disdain. It is no wonder that at both personal and policy levels, the waters of homelessness are muddied by contradictions.

Observers simply don't know what to do. My heart may go out to that homeless person sitting in the cold with a sign. but should I really give him money that he could use to buy alcohol and drugs? Should we pass laws that prevent or limit panhandling when it curbs a growing public nuisance or safety issue but criminalizes those who may be trying to climb out of homelessness? Should I ask the guy passed out on the ground if he is okay when he might be dangerous or unstable? Should I call the police? Do nothing? Should I personally pay for a homeless woman's night at a motel? Should my city subsidize housing for people who live on the street when many others work two jobs to afford their rent? It depends on which narrative about the homeless I choose to invoke, and whatever I choose, there is its persuasive opposite.

Invisibility and Super-visibility

One product of this self-contradictory perception, seen with homeless eyes, is that one feels either super-visible or invisible. Homeless individuals complained of both in my interviews. *"Can you believe it?"* Kevin asked me. *"They arrested me for sleeping too long in the forest. Do you know anyone else arrested for camping out?"* The same super-visibility issue was apparent in Ross's exchange with the police officer, recounted earlier in the chapter, and with Malcolm, a forest dweller and day laborer helping Jason understand how camping sites were selected.

When Malcolm led Jason into the forest to show him his campsite, someone called the police. Although camping in the area was legal, the police investigated, and much to Jason's chagrin, it turned out that his homeless research partner had an outstanding arrest warrant for violation of parole. (Much of the time when this happens, as in this case, the charge is failure to report on time to the parole officer, and, as you will see in chapter 5, the logistical challenges of reporting are partially to blame.) He was arrested on the spot, leaving Jason to refigure how and where he should talk with homeless participants in his research. Although Malcolm was released the following day, and Jason drove to the jail to pick him up, Malcolm had already missed the transport bus to the pumpkin-picking job in New Mexico he had just secured.

The problem of visibility goes beyond attracting the eyes of the police. It cuts to the heart of identity, and the basic wish not to be, in current parlance, "othered." One morning, after Ross had already secured a semi-permanent subsidized room at a Motel 6, he asked me, *"Tell me the truth: Do I look homeless?"*

"Why are you asking me that?" I responded.

He proceeded to relate the story of his morning. Ross's motel was just a few blocks from a Super Walmart, where he could buy food for his room, which he had outfitted with makeshift shelving and an illegal hotplate. Ross had walked the couple of blocks, bought provisions, and was returning on foot with two full plastic Walmart shopping bags. Ross continued, *"I'm walking along the road back to my room—just walking, you know, carrying Walmart bags, and this . . . Indian guy comes over to me and hands me five dollars. Can you believe it? I was just walking on the road with food I had bought. So that's why I'm asking. Do I look like I'm homeless? Like I need help?"*

It was a heart-wrenching question. It didn't matter much what my answer would be.

The pain of being noticed as different is often better than not being noticed at all. Pedestrians walk by a homeless person in a doorway without a glance; drivers avert their eyes from curbside panhandlers, in part from guilt, in part to avoid raising hopes that some donation will be forthcoming. On a website begun by once homeless Mark Horvath, the videographer and activist tells what probably is an apocryphal story (beginning "I once heard a story about") of a homeless man on Hollywood Boulevard who was handed a Christian pamphlet. "What!" the story reads, "You can see me?" The man, so long ignored like "a piece of trash on the sidewalk," felt that he had become invisible.

The Invisible People website (invisiblepeople.tv) presents the first names, faces, voices, and stories of numerous homeless individuals. You can watch short unedited videos in which homeless participants describe their lives in their own words. They are worth watching. The narratives offer the public a window into the lives of homeless individuals and a forum for dozens of people to tell their stories. They are presented in the hope of affecting the daily interactions that these and many more homeless individuals experience.

Part of the problem when you meet a homeless person is that there is no personal history. There is a tired face, or an alcoholic gaze, or an injured presence that makes you either turn away or offer spare change. This is not Charlie or Ruth. You don't know what this person looked like as a child. Or what his mother did for the community, or how well he could sing, or where his family lived.

There are few channels available to a homeless person to be "known" in any full human sense. Unless you are homeless yourself, it is unlikely that you would know a homeless person's name, much less anything of her family, her history, her talents, or her life situation before she was sleeping on a park bench, or living at a shelter, or seeking a handout.

For a homeless individual, daily contact with the non-homeless public, beyond a smile exchanged with a patron offering a dollar or two, comes through institutions, with people whose job it is to relate to the homeless. How one is known is always sifted through the set roles of the shelter, the food bank, the church, the free clinic, the probation office, or the charity organization. Chapters 4 and 7 delve into those interactions in further depth. In most other daily interactions, a homeless person will be either invisible or anonymous. It's why when something other than that occurs, it can be so poignant.

I met Miriam, a fifty-something African American woman, when I volunteered in a church shelter set up to handle the overflow of patrons who flock to the shelters in the cold winter months.

It was Miriam whom I saw sniffing the bedding, which she would afterward drag into a separate room—really an office—where the women slept. One of my roles there, besides organizing food and coffee for the patrons, was to welcome people and talk to them as they were settled for the night.

Most interactions between church workers and homeless clients had a scripted quality. *"Welcome! There's coffee on the small table, and help yourself to snacks over there. Nice to see you tonight!"* The tone was friendly but superficial. The homeless, arriving for the night with their gear and boxes of bedding, typically returned the greeting, and many would voice a "thank you" for the food and the effort as they staked out their places on the floor.

"Hi, where are you coming from?" I asked Miriam in that friendly volunteer way after she had sat down with her beverage. *"Pennsylvania"* was her answer. *"Oh? I came from there too. I lived in Philadelphia. What about you?"* I asked to extend a show of interest. Miriam shared that her clerical job and her life with her (now estranged) husband had been nearby there, but she added, *"Well, actually I'm from here."*

"Really?" I said with surprise, because it was not usual in my experience to encounter homeless who grew up in the town. And our conversation took a new path about how she happened to leave and return, and then where she had lived in town, where she had gone to school. Within a few minutes more, we were into a *"Do you know this place? This person?"* conversation.

We talked back and forth now about our lives, and it was in this context that Miriam mentioned her childhood, her grandfather, an important figure in her life, and her experiences growing up in our town. Almost an hour had gone by when I realized that I was the only volunteer still in the church for the night, having been absorbed in the conversation. *"It was so nice talking with you,"* she said, and I felt the same. Something in Miriam's conversation tweaked my memory. It was the name of her grandfather, which I recognized. With a little research, I found that, sure enough, her grandfather had been part of an oral history project whose interviews I had listened to years ago to get my cultural and historical bearings after moving to town. I went to the library and listened to the tapes again, to Miriam's grandfather talking about his life—how he came from the South in pursuit of better wages and a better life; how he raised a family that included Miriam's mother, and other details of what probably was Miriam's early life.

When I saw Miriam again at the church's makeshift shelter and she headed in my direction, I wondered whether to say anything at all. Was this too personal? A violation of her privacy? Something she would want left unknown? I decided, because of the details she had shared the night before, to ask the question: *"Is the grandfather you told me about the same man who came here from ———?"* (I named the town and the state.)

Her mouth opened in visible surprise. *"How do you know that?"*

"He was interviewed thirty years ago," I began.

"Yes! Yes!" she interjected excitedly, clearly cognizant of the tapes.

"Well . . . I listened to those tapes at the library, I heard him talk about his brothers and his sisters, and his children, how he would go hunting in the woods."

She took my hand. *"Yes, that's him, I would go squirrel hunting with him as a child!"* she exclaimed. *"I can't believe you know my grandfather."*

There was a look between us that I will never forget. It was a look of being recognized.

People Like Us

"Please always remember," the last sentence begins on the "About Us" page of the Invisible People website, "the homeless people you'll ignore today were much like you not so long ago." The words remind us that what we are missing in the perception of homeless individuals is how "like us" they are.

It is an omission one can notice in the freelist adjectives. Although descriptors like Aggressiveness and Mental Instability that invite alarm are far different from those like Neediness and Frailty that invite our pity, neither alternative is "like us." Neither suggests a relationship of sameness and equality, of mutual connection and obligation. Even descriptors such as Survivor, although nobler, suggest a breed apart. Only a few words on the freelists define qualities we would want in a neighbor (Friendly and Kind are two), but words such as "helpful" or "funny" or "generous" are noticeably absent. Missing is the message of belonging, connection, and mutual obligation that extends to "one of us."

One of the social acts that creates a sense of connection and relationship is gift giving. When gifts go in one direction, they signal an asymmetrical relationship—the giver "higher" than the receivers—as between parent and children, donors and charities, or patrons and those in need. When relationships are socially equal, the gift giving tends to be more balanced and two-way.

Even knowing all this intellectually, I missed an opportunity in my friendship with Ross, and made a thoughtless mistake. Just after Ross had moved out of the forest and into a motel room (as part of a subsidized veterans' program), he recovered a few items of value that he had placed in a storage unit. One of them was a lovely original painting, given to him by a homeless Native American artist with whom he had shared a connection and some months together in the forest.

He offered me his painting as a gift. It was really the first chance that Ross had in our years of friendship to give me something of conventional worth. I accepted the painting with thanks, but the bright orange and red acrylics on the canvas did not, I decided, mesh with my house décor. I took the painting to work, with the intention of hanging it in my office or a hallway of my university building. Given that I worked in an anthropology department, I asked my department chair, a museum curator, to appraise the painting, which she considered a very decent work, probably worth $250 to $300 and appropriate for a wall in our building.

I donated it to the department in Ross's name, and asked that a formal note of thanks that included the monetary amount of the gift be sent to Ross. I was happy a week later to see the nicely embossed card with the school logo, and the handwritten message thanking Mr. Moore for his gift. I swung by Ross's room, pleased to give him the card. He opened it with curiosity, but the minute I saw his face (and despite his *"Thanks, this is nice"* remark), I knew. I was prepared for his softly spoken *"You know, I gave it to you for you. I wanted you to have the painting. I wish you woulda wanted to keep it."*

What was I thinking? As Marcel Mauss, the French anthropologist, explained in his classic work *The Gift*, there can be no greater act of mutual obligation and connection than a gift offered and received.

The next two chapters take the reader deeper into the homeless life both in the shelters and on the street.

4

A Sheltered, Homeless Day

It is 4:05 pm and already there are twenty-plus people waiting to get into the Community Shelter when it opens at 4:30. This is a very light turnout, perhaps only a fraction of what you would see on a bone-chilling January evening. It is ninety degrees but bearable in the shade, and everyone—except for one man standing first in line and wearing a hooded jacket—has found a shaded waiting place. Most are seated on the paved parking lot, in a spot up against the wall of the shelter where a wide rectangular swath of blacktop is shadowed. Closer to the street, a small planted island with a little greenery is circled by a cement curb, and this is where, with five others, I sit too.

Those waiting talk in dyads or threes, or sit solitary, staring, sleeping, a couple looking at their phones. There are numerous backpacks on the ground; those without packs carry thin plastic supermarket bags containing bottled water, orange juice, Gatorade. One man holds a supermarket Bundt cake in a clear plastic container. Another stuffs a large bag of potato chips into his backpack as he sets it "in line." Many hold their place in the entrance line like this, with a backpack or bag or bike as proxy, so they don't have to stand in the sun. The line now has eight bicycles, six backpacks, and a handful of shopping bags.

Clearly, a few people in the waiting yard have behavioral issues. A thin, drawn woman rides by on her bicycle shouting at a woman near me on the curb. "*If you ever do that again . . . ,*" she screams. "*If you EVER do that again.*" The seated woman is smirking as she waves off the ranting rider. "*Go away,*" she says quietly, making a brushing movement with her hand. You can tell it is really *not* personal. It is not clear that the duo in the exchange even know each other well. The woman on the bike is "crazy," as I hear one man say to another spectator.

The biker pedals over to another woman across the lot, only this time her target is a person who has already made her presence known by a prior loud and heated argument in the public space. The rider begins again—"*IF you EVER . . .*"—but she is met with an even louder comeback: "*You get the fuck out of here!!*" And despite the fact that the bicyclist turns quickly to leave, the angry talker rises to her feet and runs after the bike, chasing it off the property and into the street.

Most shelter "clients" (as they are called), though, are quiet and watchful. In the last few minutes before 4:30, the lot has doubled in population. Many have moved next to their placeholders in line. Before joining the waiting line, one man carries his plastic bag to the curb, flashing a few cans, offering a woman to my left a beer. He is getting rid of his stash, I assume, before entering the gate, where alcohol is contraband, and enlisting friends and acquaintances to drink up. Although you do not need to come into the shelter sober, you cannot bring alcohol or drugs onto the property.

At 4:30 exactly, a staff woman and four men appear at the padlocked gate. The woman unlocks the chain-link entrance and stands as the gatekeeper with the gate held partially closed, while the four men stand in a row behind two long wooden tables. Everyone watches as they put on blue latex gloves. The gatekeeper opens the gate to let in four people, and each puts his pack or bag on the table. The gloved men search the bags, taking out the contents, holding some items up to the light; they open jars and bottles, and smell what is inside. Approved bags are handed back to the clients, and they continue another twenty feet to the next station, as the gatekeeper lets in a few more.

The next stop is the "bed" table. A woman sits behind a wooden table with a clipboard. In front of her is a box holding laminated cards, all facedown. You reach in and grab one. It's a lottery. *"What's your number?"* she asks. And she records the answer after verifying the numeral on your card. The number you pull determines your chances of getting a bed. Low numbers mean you will likely get a bed, maybe even a bottom bunk. A high number means that you get whatever is left: a top bunk or the floor.

A person with crutches or with a serious mobility problem—not just a sprained ankle, the shelter administrator told me—gets to "pass through" and go to the front of the line. These passes, though, are used only judiciously, and always with medical approval.

You next move to an outdoor waiting area until the shelter staff are ready to receive clients. You are called up by name in the order of the lottery number you chose. *"Henry!"* a staff member yells into the yard, as she looks at the column of names next to the list of ascending numbers on her clipboard. Henry rises from his place in the yard and enters. With only fifty-eight people on the list today, the wait for numbers to be called is shorter than usual, yet it will take almost an hour before the whole process is complete and you are lying on a bed. Even on this relatively temperate evening, clients are impatient to get inside. One man calls out, *"You passed my number. I was sixteen."* The clipboard holder, who knows most clients by name, gazes down. *"No, you're sixty."* The man shakes his head but is silent.

The intake staff member, "Anna," sits inside the shelter and is the first person you will encounter when you finally enter the door. She looks at the list of available beds, all numbered bunk beds, on her computer and tries to match your request. Your name will be input as the occupant of the bed number assigned. Most people are return clients, and their names already appear in the computer database.

"*I want a bottom bunk,*" says the first guy through the door. Anna nods in acknowledgment, her eyes still on the computer screen: "*Okay, go to bunk number twelve.*" Some regulars thank Anna by name before moving into the room to find their numbered bed. Others rummage through the small box on the intake table with travel-size soaps and shampoos, taking one or two.

Almost everyone, of course, wants a bottom bunk. There are only twenty-four bottom bunks for men and six for women, so on even a slightly busy night, the bottom bunks are quickly taken. Then top bunks are assigned. Then it is the floor. Those at the losing end of the lottery, who must sleep on the cement floor, are given two blankets, one to use as a pad and one as a cover, along with their pillow.

A thirtyish man on crutches has received a "pass" through the door. He walks clumsily with one crutch, carrying the other one along with an armful of bags he has brought. He is assigned bunk number 28, a bottom bunk.

"*Do you need help?*" I ask him as he stands there with arms loaded. He smiles at me. "*Just finding the bed.*" I'm not sure where bunk number 28 is located either, but each bed has a number taped on and I begin searching with him—walking between the labyrinthine rows of beds. We find the bed but not before a resident has instructed me—thinking I am a client too—that I shouldn't be in the men's area. The rules.

On the bed—which is unmade—is a plastic-covered mattress with a pillow, a sheet, and a blanket. Noticing it, I remember what Penelope told me—that seeing this blanket brought her to tears. "*I know I was already upset at having to be at the shelter,*" she had explained, "*but the blanket definitely made it worse. It was this, uh, 'survival' blanket. I wanted to bring a comforter from my storage area, but they say, 'Use this—it'll keep you warm.' But I thought no, I don't want that to touch me.*"

I could see what she meant. The mottled gray-brown scratchy-looking industrial bedcover, referred to as a "humanitarian blanket," is an unwoven product (70 percent polyester, 30 percent wool) of a process called needle punch, which uses a machine to separate fibers and then knot them into a shape. It is a cheap way to make a blanket.

"*I wear my onesies* [a one-piece pajama] *so none of that will touch my skin,*" Penelope continues. "*I had them on every day! Me and this other girl wear pajamas . . . I can't fall asleep without them. Everyone [else] sleeps in their clothes.*"

Women and men sleep on opposite sides of the main shelter room. The men, with the majority of beds on the left, take up most of the shelter with four rows of bunk beds going back to the wall. The women, on the right, have just one wall of twelve beds. The overflow women sleep on the floor in the administrative area, or outside if the weather is nice.

On a busy night, the shelter overflows its main room. You are lucky to have any bed at all. If you don't show up at 4:30—even if you are on crutches or in a wheelchair—you cannot be promised a bed. "*A guy in a wheelchair,*" Kyle, who runs the shelter, tells me, "*will sleep in his chair if there are no beds and he hasn't shown up when the gates open.*"

Administrators and staff are caught in a constant pull between the wants of clients and the mission and resources of the shelter.

Kyle describes the difficult issues involved in deciding who can come to the shelter: *"The person has got to be able to take care of themselves. Sometimes, somebody says. 'My friend, or my spouse, will come to help me in the bathroom.' 'Sorry, that won't work,' I tell them. You need to be able to take care of yourself."*

The rule can seem coldhearted, but Kyle explains that *"if a guy is belligerent and uncooperative—I've had it happen . . . somebody throwing punches at other clients, and they won't respond to staff. If I can't throw them out, the shelter is in a place it can't be."* Kyle was clear. *"I can't be in the place that someone is threatening others but their life would be threatened if they needed to leave."*

It is 5:40 by the time everyone is processed and in the shelter. Another eight people are already in the parking lot waiting to get in. They are "late" for the first check-in, and the gate is locked again. They will wait there until the next staff task—the outside check— is completed. Throughout the night the compound will remain locked, but a camera pointed at the entrance gate alerts staff to the presence of someone trying to get in. This shelter takes all comers who can make it through the gate on their own steam.

Oscar leads me around the yard for the "outside check" as he looks for stashed alcohol or weapons. It is booze mostly, he says, that people will try to access during the night. Once in a while there is a weapon, usually a knife. We look at the edges of the fence, where already small openings have been patched. He looks in the garbage, shows me a little bag attached to a bike (a likely hiding place), and inside the wheel hubs of the minibuses on the shelter property that in winter take the overflow population to cooperating churches.

Inside, people make their beds, unpack their belongings, and use the bathroom. There are two "private" bathrooms, one unisex and one for women, each with a single toilet and sink designed for one patron at a time. The bathroom is available when the key is in the open box on the front desk. It is a standard door key, but it is attached to two iron shelf brackets (or door hinges?) that have been bolted together to make the key weigh a couple of pounds. This way, no one could easily lose the key, steal the key, forget to return the key, or leave it in the door. The women's shower is also private, accessed with another formidable key, but the men's shower is communal, and often the subject of criticism by clients. The larger men's bathroom includes multiple sinks, urinals, stalls, and a shower and remains unlocked.

The most noticeable thing about the bathrooms to an outsider is the toilet paper. A heavy-gauge length of chain hangs like a necklace from a metal attachment on the wall. The chain is strung through three toilet paper rolls, two on one side of the loop, one on the other. The two ends of the chain are joined together with a padlock. The staff alone has that key, so that patrons cannot abscond with the toilet tissue in their backpacks.

Safety, mission, and resources (like toilet paper) all constantly figure into the daily rules of the shelter. Keeping to the rules becomes increasingly important as the number of clients grows from a night when almost everyone gets a bed to a night in the winter when freezing temperatures drive many more to the shelter.

When the numbers are more than the shelter can hold, local churches step in to handle the overflow population. The shelter staff pick carefully from their "known" clients, soliciting those who are quiet, respectful, and sober to send to a church and their volunteer greeters. Clients say they like to go to the churches, where there might be a DVD movie, extra snacks, and a welcoming band of outside volunteers. But going to the church also means no beds—you sleep on the floor—and shelter staff may need to

sweeten the call for volunteers with guarantees of future bottom
bunk assignments at the shelter.

Dinner is at 6. Clients know the schedule and, several minutes
before dinner is served, a waiting line forms that stretches across
the room, all along the men's sleeping area and sometimes out the
shelter door. The food for the shelter is set up on two tables. Tonight I serve
desserts, all packaged from the supermarket. Some have discounted prices on them, showing that they were dated and the
store was reducing the price. There are two Bundt-shaped cakes,
vanilla with a rose tint, that say "Strawberry" on the box. There
are two round layer cakes, one with thick vanilla icing and one
with chocolate. Two peach pies and four apple pies, of two different brands, complete the dessert table. Clients come and tell
me what they want, and I serve with a blunt cake knife that must
be returned to the kitchen before people self-serve their seconds.
Dessert, I am to realize months later, is not usual fare.

Pork ribs with beans. A casserole dish with carrots and potatoes.
Three kinds of bread. A salad of mixed lettuce and a fresh fruit
salad. These make up the main meal. Clients are served by multiple
helpers, a combination of staff and both outside and client volunteers. (This night, Ally does the bread and salads. I do desserts.
Niko does the main course.) The food comes directly from the
local food bank in metal thermal containers with doors that reveal
shelves that hold the trays.

There are drinks but no cups—so there is really no way to serve
beverages. I see Niko washing plastic spoons and forks (turned
in from a previous meal) so there will be enough for dinner. The
resources are variable like this. Food is typically reliable, but other
items, like plates, cups, and plastic ware, are not.

Once everyone is served, some dishes are removed, the others consolidated into a "seconds" area, squeezed onto one table. For a little while longer, before all the food is cleared away, clients can serve themselves from the food still remaining.

By 6:45, dinner is over, and there is a shout-out to the main room and the yard: *"Storage!" "Storage!"* People begin stirring from their after-dinner places, moving toward the room-size metal bin that sits on the property. They know they will have only fifteen minutes. Once in the morning, and once now, they are able to access their suitcases, plastic bags, duffels, and backpacks—anything other than the one book sized bag and one grocery bag allowed inside the shelter.

Storage visits are supervised to protect everyone's belongings, so clients must go into the storage room, remove their bag or container, and show their name (which must be written on the item) to a staff member. Owners place the bags on a table and rifle through to find the items they need for the night or the morning—tomorrow's change of clothes, toiletries for bedtime, the book that they'll read until they fall asleep—and then return the bags with the same check of their names.

The quick end to "storage access" begins cleaning time. Everyone, except those clients who signed up for a cleaning job, must leave the shelter building—regardless of weather. The sign-up sheet with jobs and adjacent spaces to enter your name sits on the entrance table, and the staff checks to see if these unpaid and unperked jobs are filled. Usually clients come forward to sweep, mop, clean the bathrooms and showers, take out the trash to the Dumpsters. But sometimes it takes an insistent *"I need more volunteers"* before all jobs are covered.

By 8 pm, with floors cleaned, the temporary beds for those who didn't manage a bunk bed in the lottery are laid out in rows along the concrete floor. This is one of my jobs. I am instructed that the eighty-by-sixty-two-inch humanitarian blanket must be folded twice lengthwise to produce a fourfold "mattress" layer. This increases the cushioning the blanket provides while saving floor space, but it also means that the bed footprint a client encounters is a scanty-looking twenty inches wide. And it is just over five feet in length, leaving most clients' lower limbs resting on the concrete floor. *"Do you have a mattress?"* one client asks. *"A mattress?"* Anna repeats with a puzzled look. The client understands the answer is no. Clients go to their beds quickly because there is little room to move around inside the shelter, and no real social space. Lights are out by 10 pm.

Lights come on again at the shelter at 5 am. Few are happy with the early wake-up. When I arrive at 5:30, some people are already walking out through the gate. Others are in line for breakfast—today, coffee and hard-boiled eggs.

Those finished with breakfast are stripping their beds. Because the shelter is intentionally not offered as "home," the bed that a client has just slept in is not her bed. Even if she plans on returning this evening, she will go through the same process of bed assignment, and be issued new bedding.

Two piles, one of blankets, one of sheets and pillowcases, mushroom in size on the floor as clients trudge over to the piling area with their armfuls of bedding. Compliance is rarely a problem. If you fail to strip your bed, staff explain to me, you lose your right to a bed. If you return, you sleep on the floor. If clients used a locker (for which they must provide their own lock), they must remove their items daily. They leave the shelter with everything not locked up outside in the storage unit.

Client volunteers, who are permitted to stay in the shelter during the day, will wash and dry the sheets and cases, and put the blankets in a hot dryer to "disinfect" them. (The shelter has already endured its first case of bedbugs.) As one staffer tells me, this is the "heavy lifting" time of day for workload, when floors are swept and mopped, toilets and showers cleaned.

Some people return to their bare mattresses to get a few more minutes of sleep before they are ushered out of the shelter; others use the time to take a shower or check their mail. Three different people come up to the desk to grab a big plastic bottle of liquid soap/shampoo (which, I assume from client behavior, must remain on the desk). One woman squirts a dollop onto her hair and leaves. One man lathers up his hair at the desk before heading for a bathroom sink, while another squeezes a handful of the liquid into his cupped hand as he moves gingerly toward the shower area. Showers are timed, and the posted sign says they must be kept under fifteen minutes.

Getting a bath towel for showering involves another clipboard with numbers. Each towel handed out has a number, and you "sign out" your towel. After your shower, you return the towel, initial the clipboard to show that you returned it, and have a staff member also initial the return. All who neglect to return their towels will be denied a fresh bath towel the following week, when their names will show up on a printed roster.

Disposable items, from aspirin and Band-Aids to toiletries, are simply given out, if they are available. Two women come to the desk for Q-tips. A guy wants a razor. There is a request for an ibuprofen, but acetaminophen is the closest alternative. Another woman wants a comb but there is none—the shelter is out.

This is also the time when a number of clients check their mail. It is an important service of the shelter that it provides a street address where people can have their mail sent. The mail is kept in a locked cabinet in alphabetical folders. *"Do I have mail?"* asks one man looking for a check from a bail bondsman that may be coming, and staff must go through all of the envelopes in the lettered folder to check. The scores of envelopes in each folder almost all appear official; it is not usually personal mail that people get here. These are communications from offices of probation, courts, legal and medical offices, and government programs such as Social Security, Medicaid, and Veteran Affairs.

"*I was told,*" one guy says politely, "*that I can have my knife back now.*" He waits. His knife is locked in a special secure cabinet where contraband items taken at the entrance are housed. The person with the right key comes and opens the cabinet, returning his knife. The client must now leave the grounds immediately, escorted out the gate. That's the rule.

Rules matter. As clients prepare to leave, one man (with gear on his back ready to leave) spots Kyle. The client has been "sanctioned" because of an incident of loud, rowdy behavior. Although he is allowed in the shelter, he can only come after 10 pm to get his bed.

"*Why do I keep having to come then?*" the man complains.

"*Because you didn't show up for your appointment to talk about what happened. Anytime between ten and two any weekday. You know what you have to do—come in and we talk about what happened and then we'll see what we can do.*"

Kyle explains that this is how he deals with inappropriate behavior at the shelter. The person involved in an incident must come in the next day, when it is often inconvenient for the client, requiring effort. He will need to talk about the incident and take responsibility for his actions. If the person doesn't show, or he shows and says he did nothing wrong, then the sanction stays.

A young man on his way out the door hails Will, a staff member. "*Hey! I'll see you at nine am,*" he shouts, smiling. "*I'm gonna get some clothes. I have a job interview!!*" It's clear he is proud, and Will shouts back his encouragement, publicly. *"Way to go, Scott. You'll be looking sharp!"* From 9 am to 1 pm, clients can come in through a different door—because the dormitory end of the shelter is technically closed—and request a supervised visit in the "shop." There they can pick out items of (donated) clothing they need. Scott will shop for his interview clothes later today, and I am told they have a healthy supply of ties.

It is 7:20 am, time to leave. In the main room, people are lingering. Some seem almost to be hiding by their stillness and silence, but the staff watches. Will goes over and wakes up an unmoving figure curled on a mattress and jostles two others nearby who are still lying down.

At the front desk, a staff member cups his hands to direct his shouted announcement, *"Time to leave! Building is closing!"* He repeats it. He must walk over to a lone woman on a corner bed to instruct her to leave. She will move to the yard in the shade, but she knows that she will need to leave there too within a half hour. People reluctantly exit the shelter, some giving dirty looks or grimaces on the way out. *"Did you see the look he gave me?"* Will says to me with a smile and a shake of his head. A chicken salad sandwich, the offering of the day, is distributed to everyone leaving, but there are (to my surprise) only a few takers.

Shelter staff—many of whom have been in dire circumstances themselves in their lives—vary widely in their personal styles, specifically the degree of easiness, open empathy, and affability they show to clients. Kyle sees this as a positive, a way of encouraging clients to develop interactional skills with different kinds of people and authorities.

Most shelter staff are sympathetic to the early departure schedules, especially in bad weather and in the cold months. *"In the winter,"* Oscar shares, *"it can be freezing. Sometimes new people don't realize they have to leave. They have no clothing or anything. Even though we're not supposed to let them 'shop' upstairs for clothes except certain hours, we find them things."* Years after being homeless, Cal, now working with homeless at a nonprofit agency, still remembers vividly being pushed out the door into a freezing morning from a different shelter. *"God—it's just barbaric, especially Sundays and holidays, because there's nothing open and nowhere to go."*

Still, the policy goes back to mission, to what shelters are there for. As one shelter staff member put it, *"This is not a hotel. It's not a long-term place to stay. It is people's choice to stay here, and it shouldn't be made too comfortable."*

"Can you really say that people have a choice to be here?" I questioned.

"Yes," was his quick response. *"Most of the people here have some kind of income. They just don't want to spend their income on rent. It's a choice."*

"But is it a choice," I press, *"when rents here are so high?"*

"Absolutely," he answered assuredly. *"They could choose to live somewhere else."*

The first day of the month, when people receive their government checks, perhaps best demonstrates homeless exercise of "choice." The first days of any month are consistently when the shelters are less full. Many homeless will use a portion of their monthly income to pay for a night, even a week (at the discounted weekly rate), at a motel, where their room, their shower, and their schedule are their own.

It is 7:45 am. Vacating the shelter property every morning involves more than dealing with the early hour or the weather; for most homeless, it means dealing with the public, and with public perceptions about who they are. In a business across the way, where employees are at work at this early hour, they can look out the window toward the shelter. *"You know what we say?"* an employee shares with me. *"There they go . . . the zombies."*

Clients leaving the shelter have no choice but to walk, unless they are among the few with their own vehicle. There is no bus route to or from the shelter. And they are walking with all their "stuff," which cannot be left in the shelter. It is about a mile to the main road, and about the same to the bus stop. The shortest distance to a business other than the one across the street is a little over a mile. It is a four-and-a-half-mile walk to the center of town, a half-hour walk to the Safeway or the enclosed shopping mall, which doesn't open until 10 am.

Both of the nearer businesses, Will tells me, have become stricter about letting homeless people stay on their property. The mall posts this official "code of conduct" rule on its website, prohibiting visitors from *"loitering, delaying, lingering, or remaining idle at the —————— Mall without any useful business for being present."*

"So, where can people go that is indoors?" I ask.

"They go to the library. On Sunday, there is a school they go where there is a service. Not too many places," Will estimates.

"You should see the Burger King people when all the homeless come," Penelope tells me in an interview. The Burger King is one of the closest commercial establishments by foot, and it opens early, at 6 am.

"Sometimes," she explains, using the third person, *"they don't buy anything but water. So the Burger King people get mad. They get more madder when all of them have the crown on—the Burger King crown,"* meaning the paper crown given out to customers, usually children. *"There'll be like nine people with the Burger King crown on and they're all homeless. They're all drinking water, right? Yeah, like they buy one cup of coffee, and you get one refill, that's all."* Then

she switches to the first person. *"Sometimes I think they expect us to leave. But then we don't."*

Penelope openly laughs as she visualizes the picture she's describing. *"So, there we are, and everyone has asked for a Burger King crown, which is free. So there are nine homeless people sitting at their table with one coffee and their waters and their crowns. And they'll say, 'Okay, you guys. You can't get more of the Burger King hats.'"*

People who cannot get themselves to the library or to a receptive place of business can be seen ambling on or near shelter grounds. Today, a man on crutches has crossed the street and is sitting on a rock under a tree. Another woman has stretched out a blanket under a different tree, with phone, purse, water, and jacket laid neatly in her sight. I see her move her position, and her possessions, as the angle of the sun changes. Two other clients, there the night before, have found shade under the eaves of the building and are lying on blankets along the entrance path to the door, which stays open between 10 am and 2 pm for those who want to register at the shelter, talk to Kyle about an incident or a plan for the future, see a nurse or a social worker. Both of the reclining figures, one man and one woman, tuck themselves close to the building so that those entering will not need to literally step over them. It will be more than six hours before they and the others can return inside, to begin the cycle again.

The Pros and Cons of Shelter Life

Talk to enough homeless people and you will find out what makes one shelter different from another. In one, you must go to a religious service to stay the night. At another, someone can help you with your résumé in addition to providing a bed and a meal. That one won't let you in if you're drunk or smell of alcohol.

There may be different rules about the number of days you can stay, whether you need to pay $5 for the night, or whether you can come with a pet. Some are bigger, cleaner, or more convenient.

But there is also something familiar about a shelter as an institution, no matter its design, size, and services. To anyone who frequents shelters, it is an institution with a common feel, with well-known pros and cons. And while I draw my descriptions largely, but not completely, from one shelter, the day described has a reality that will be recognizable to most who have slept at a shelter.

Most clients will tell you that the shelter lent them a helping hand, often at a time of crisis. It "gave me a place to stay when I needed it most," writes one client rating this shelter on the Internet, while another expresses gratitude for being allowed to "stop by for showers every few days during a rough time." Some offer only faint praise, like "better than freezing outside, breakfast and supper served daily." But "how do you rate a place," asks another client, "where people down on their luck gather?" A warm bed, food, and a shower are the most frequent foci of gratefulness, but the Community Shelter also provides an address to register to vote or receive official mail, a place to get needed clothing, and an avenue to connect with social and health service programs.

Every year, on December 21, the longest night of the year, the shelter's director and others in the community light candles and read the names of the local homeless people who died during the year. Between 2014 and 2017, in our small city of fewer than 75,000, a disturbing forty-five homeless people died. The Community Shelter has contributed to a recent decrease in deaths due to exposure, but the homeless are still dying from illness and overdoses and from violent attacks; in our town, most are killed by drivers of cars or trains who did not realize they were there. Nationally, deaths of homeless have soared.

Most of these deaths come from among the homeless population who were not using a public or private shelter. One of the more recent deaths even occurred on shelter grounds. This is why Yolanda, on staff, tells me she goes out every night with a partner to do a search of the area, checking the outer grounds of the shelter and also the open fields, a nearby drainage ditch, even venturing into the precarious tunnels that run under the highway. Sometimes they find people. Why a homeless person would remain unsheltered, particularly in the dead of a northern winter or the heat of a southern summer—that can seem baffling . . . until you ask homeless people.

Number one, they chafe at the rules. Jerald, who came to the shelter after a short stint of incarceration, said it felt the same as jail. When to get up; when to eat; how long to shower. Wendi told me that most shelters *"treat you either like children or cattle."* Part of the problem too, for some, is the perception that the rules don't seem to apply to everyone equally. It was a recurring complaint that staff or client volunteers, each with some measure of power, *"played favorites."* Some gripes, though, were less dependent on the eye of the beholder: in some shelters you can't bring your dog; in most shelters you can't sleep with your spouse. Married people must split up and sleep separately, on men's and women's sides. For some, the problem can be simply that you can't drink.

Grumbles about shelter life typically become more frequent when the facility is overcrowded, trying to serve more people than its resources allow. Waiting lines are longer. Ending up on the top bunk or the floor is more likely. There is less personal space. Showers must be kept shorter. A second portion, or even a first, of some favorite food might not be available. Mostly, though, clients understand the constraints of crowding, and these kinds of complaints are not what singularly move people into the forests and streets.

The most pointed objections to shelter life involve people's sense of personal safety and control, with many concerns focused on other shelter clients. Outsiders must be reminded that a wide swath of circumstances explains one's presence at a shelter. When I began volunteering at the shelter, I was touched, really, that Anna cared enough to ask me if I had a place to stay that night. A staff member, with many years' experience, was worried that I was homeless and not declaring it. Her compassion jolted my sense of "us" and "them," reminding me of the fragility of all our lives and the diverse people and circumstances addressed by shelters.

On any given night, one client is stumbling drunk, needing help to get into bed, while another has just been evicted despite her full-time job and cannot find housing right away that she is able to afford. In the upper bunk of one bed is a drunk driver whose trailer, in which he was living, has been impounded, while the older man in the bottom bunk, on Social Security, was camping in the forest when it was suddenly closed due to fire danger. One woman ruminates to a friend before entering the shelter about how she will score her drug of choice the next day, while another, who climbs into bed by 8:15 pm, shares her worries with me about falling asleep early so she will be rested for her 6 am job at a fast food restaurant. An "everybody-knows-it" heroin addict sleeps in a bed next to a man on pain medication with nowhere to go in a strange town following surgery at the regional hospital. There are those teetering on the edge of mental illness alongside others who are stranded after moving here for a job that fell through. A young man, newly released from prison for a crime he is "uncomfortable sharing about," will perhaps stand in the food line behind a woman fleeing an abusive relationship.

I have met each of these people, albeit on several different nights at the shelter, and will tell you that there are only a couple I didn't personally like (and which ones they were might surprise you). Still, it is no stretch to imagine that many clients worry about their "stuff," or have ongoing issues of trust about the company they are keeping. *"Can you believe,"* Cal asks me rhetorically, *"that people with almost nothing would steal from others with almost nothing?"* Despite clear circles of camaraderie among clients, one hears frequent complaints that their property gets stolen by other shelter users. Even locked storage at the shelters has its risks if anyone leaves an item in a locker or storage area. The sign says "Items Will Be Thrown Out If Not Reclaimed"—an additional reminder that, in one way or another, you are not in control.

Some people are willing to put up with the limitations of shelter life for its benefits, others because the alternatives seem unthinkable. When I asked Miriam whether she had ever stayed outside the shelters, she shook her head in a definite no. *"I don't know anything about camping. . . . How am I supposed to live here without a place?—I'll freeze to death. That's why I go to the shelter even though it's not so nice."*

For others, though, the negatives simply outweigh the positives. The reason to avoid a shelter might be as blatantly obvious as the prohibition on active drinking, but it also might be much less transparent, as in the case of Joseph. He suffers from alcoholism but had been sober for many months. He just didn't want to be around alcohol and drugs and people still involved with them. Being in a shelter, he felt, would surround him with people and temptations that could lead him astray. *"It's a healthier life for me,"* he explained, *"in the forest."*

5

On the Street

Every year, the U.S. Department of Housing and Urban Development (HUD) enlists communities and agencies that want to receive federal funding to "count the homeless." On one predesignated day, the same throughout the country, a "point-in-time" (PIT) survey is conducted that takes a snapshot of homelessness in the United States. Everyone counts on the same day.

They count two main groups that fit HUD's homeless definition. The first consists of "those staying in a privately or publicly operated shelter," including those given a voucher to stay overnight in a "welfare" motel room. They do not count as homeless those who pay out of pocket for the same motel room because they cannot afford the first and last month's rent or utility down payments necessary for an apartment. Neither do they define as homeless those sleeping on the floors or couches of friends and relatives, who (statistically) will soon be on the streets.

They also conduct a tally of unsheltered homeless people—informally called the "street count"—who are at once most visible to the public but who also can be the most difficult to find. HUD defines this population as "an individual or family with a primary nighttime residence that is a public or private place not designed for or ordinarily used as a regular sleeping accommodation for human beings."

The "unsheltered" life includes a wide swath of living situations, from sidewalks and tunnels to parks and forests to bus and train stations to cars and vans and more. To count this population is challenging, which is why HUD puts out a 117-page guide about how to do this. In practice, it involves census takers traipsing into drainage ditches and tunnels, knocking on car doors, combing through likely areas of the forest—often at night. It is also why the National Law Center on Homelessness and Poverty says the unsheltered are often severely undercounted, and that the actual numbers could be many times higher.

The Annual Homelessness Assessment Report for 2018 showed that 65 percent of homeless people were in shelters, and 35 percent lived in unsheltered settings. In 2017, homelessness increased for the first time in seven years on account of a 9 percent increase in *unsheltered* homelessness; it increased again in 2018.

Although federal data and reports tend to divide the homeless world into sheltered and unsheltered, these labels obscure the fluidity between street and shelter. Ask a homeless person, and most will tell you that they have lived in more than one homeless situation. About half of those who come into a shelter (one national report put it at 46.7 percent) came from an unsheltered location. Many lead lives in which various types of sheltered and unsheltered options are interwoven.

Ross is a good example. At different points Ross has "couch surfed" with his wife's relatives, spent nights in a shelter, lived in a subsidized "welfare" motel, and camped in the forest—sometimes within the same few months. Even on a single day, in many homeless lives the street and the shelter intertwine.

If you look at the road outside the Community Shelter any day of the week, you will see a number of parked vehicles, mostly older models. Today, a Monday well into the morning, there are seven that seem likely homeless habitats. Two are compact cars that have been there a few days. A van painted gray and spotted with large patches of rust sits with its curbside sliding door open. A lone woman, who looks fiftyish and is sleeping on the backseat floor, raises her head as my car approaches; she shuts the sliding door. In front of her is a dilapidated motor home with balding tires, windows covered; then an aging two-toned black-and-white van with "Just Married," its letters now looking ragged, written across a window. On the other side of the street is an old GMC truck with a satellite dish in its open cab and a dated Wilderness trailer—windows cardboard covered—in tow. A block away is a newer Honda van, with blue plastic substituting for the side window; a tarp is stretched from the top of the parked van to a grassy location past the sidewalk, where it provides a makeshift tent for the occupants. They all live on the street—literally—but close to the shelter, making use of food handouts and even medical assistance.

Alonzo lives in his car and takes pride when he tells me that he has a full-time job, working the nightshift. Working forty hours a week, though, is not enough to pay for an apartment, so his car is his residence for the time being. With no timed parking restrictions around the shelter, he often keeps it there during the day. Alonzo's biggest problem has been finding a place in the town where he can shower before dressing for work. A local hotel will allow him to shower there for $12, but this is too much for him to pay every day. He tells me that he is considering finding a cheap membership at a health club, but for now he comes daily to the shelter.

Richard is living in an undeveloped wooded area behind a Walmart and bikes every day to work. He uses the shelter as a resource on his way to work, to shower and change, and on his way home from work, to get some food, charge his cell phone, and get a new pair of clean, dry socks. A working person can easily miss the hot meal served at the food kitchen between 4 and 5:30 pm. But he is in time for the 6 pm shelter meal. Richard eats and runs, preferring the freedom—to come and go, to drink or not—at his makeshift urban camp.

Each day there are a number of visitors to the shelter like him, who come for a giveaway sandwich, a full evening meal, a shower, or an item of clothing. With summer "monsoon season" rains, as they are called, now in progress, there are boxes of thin rain ponchos for the taking that many unsheltered homeless will come to get.

Finding Your Spot

Statistically, most homeless veterans like Ross "choose" an unsheltered life. Often averse to the restrictive rules that shelters impose, they find that living outside is the lesser evil. As Ross explained,

All this started after the service. I don't know for a fact but a lot of it I attribute to Vietnam. I wasn't ready to be a civilian again and didn't know how to act. Because I had a camping background, it kept me from sleeping on park benches and whatever. Whether that was a step better, I don't know.

"The first thing you're thinking about," he tells me, "is where can I go to that I'm secure, and I can sleep at night. A campsite, if you're homeless, that's . . . that's probably the best place you can go." Camping trumps the street in his view because "if you're living on the street, you're continually harassed by the cops because the business owners don't want any of that."

"What do you think of," I asked Ross, "when you choose a campsite?"

He paused a moment, then laughed. *"Location, location, location."* I laughed too.

The most important "location" variables, I was to learn, involve legality and visibility. Generally, homeless are looking to find a spot that will not cause them to run afoul of the law and will keep them out of clear sight of the public. Many homeless people, particularly in cities, worry more about their safety from the public than from other homeless. If there is some shelter from the weather, too, then you've found the perfect place. This is the advantage of tunnels and the space under bridges for city dwellers. It provides shelter from the elements and remains out of public view, so often the police leave people alone.

Sometimes finding a place is harder than you might think. Randy's 2008 red Chevy Cobalt SS turbo coupe, with silver-spoked hubcaps and a racing fin on the back, is filled with clothing and papers, bags and boxes. The only open space is the driver's seat and a little area in back of the seat so it can recline. This is where Randy sleeps.

Except for a single swatch where the paint has faded, the car looks well tended. Randy thinks this is why, despite signs saying that you can't park overnight, no one bothers him in his parking space in a remote area of a mall parking lot. He keeps his car clean on the outside, and it is a later model, different from the gray-and-black-paint-patched old van with no hubcaps he points out parked in a nearby space. *"They'll notice that,"* he advises me.

Randy has lived here for almost two years. *"You are best off,"* he informs me, *"on property that is private, where the owners don't notice or won't call in the law."* Parking on the streets was a problem, he explained, because, even if you find a place with no meters or parking restrictions, the police catch you if you're sleeping in your car.

Randy left the Midwest for California during the recession in search of a better climate and a job paying a decent wage. Then he got bladder cancer, *"probably,"* he tells me, *"from all the drywall work I did. They told me I could go back to work in six months after the surgery but it didn't work out that way."* I did not ask why it didn't work out. Refusing chemotherapy, Randy is hopeful that the cancer is gone. *"But some days,"* he admits, *"I don't have enough energy to get out of my car."* Financially, he stays afloat through food stamps and panhandling.

Randy counseled me as if I were his student. Not all shopping mall lots are equal, he lectured. Some are owned by the city and therefore patrolled by the local police; other lots are owned by private parties or corporations, and the police don't have jurisdiction there, unless they are called in by store or mall owners. The latter is where you want to park.

There's a lot to learn. It took some time for Jerald to learn the ropes of camping. When the last shelter where Jerald was staying closed, he had no alternative but to camp. *"I liked camping as a kid,"* he told me.

> *You know, I enjoyed that, but I never thought that I would have to use that as a means of living.*
>
> *I didn't know where to go. I mean, nobody really told me what their standards were for camping, so I literally had to kind of just go out and find my own spots and then start asking questions: "Well is this spot okay?" And the thing that I was told is that I can't stay within the city limits 'cause camping within city limits is illegal.*

The penalty for violating camping restrictions is not always just a minor slap on the wrist with an admonition to move on. For many it results in fines they cannot pay, leading to further legal problems. For repeat offenders it can even mean prison time. So homeless squatters, whether in public parks and streets or in national forests, must be careful about the sites they choose and how long they stay, because most have time restrictions too.

Jerald, who had recently been released from prison, was particularly concerned about keeping himself legal. In an attempt to stay within the letter of the law, he moved to public land about seven miles outside the city but has to bike into town every day for his job, for mandatory checks with his probation officer, for drug tests, and for required classes. Jerald is one of more than two thousand people in the county convicted of a crime who are in "intensive probation" with terms that include remaining crime-free, performing community service, undergoing substance abuse treatment, and paying restitution and court fees, along with a variety of other sanctions in lieu of prison time, or in exchange for reduced time. He negotiates all of his responsibilities from his forest camp, using the shelter to get mail, store important papers, take showers, and get an occasional giveaway sandwich.

"*I get some stuff from the shelter,*" Jerald explains, "*but basically the—it's a donation of peanut butter and jelly sandwiches on a daily basis and that gets a little old, and I guess there was times I wish we had, you know, maybe even hot food would be nice.*" Cooking in the forest is often prohibited because of the danger of fire, so his food is usually cold, and it can't be saved for the next day. He learned that the hard way when animals chewed through his tent for leftover food.

"*If I take any food home,*" he declared, "*it's always what I'm going to eat then and there.*"

Home? I noticed the word "home" in his statement. "*What did you mean by that?*" I asked.

"*My camp, my tent. That's home,*" he answered. He went on:

*It's four walls and a roof. You know, I have my own bedding and every-
thing. It's mine and it doesn't belong to anybody else. That's entirely my
own, my own thing there . . . And that's what makes it home. And I take
care of it, like I said, and—I try not to let anything happen to it or let
anybody else use it that I know that could ruin it or anything so . . . So, to
me that's home.*

Home can be a tentative and uncertain place when you are
homeless, though, a place that Ross says you *"don't make too much
out of."* For instance, *"you can't keep much there,"* he stresses, *"because who knows when your situation will change?"* Indeed, Jerald's
"home" is never that for long when he is staying on public land,
because overnight camping is allowed for only up to fourteen con-
secutive days—so homeless campers have to live light and keep
moving. As Jerald recounted:

*I think this is like my third campsite that I've moved from. Because the
first two, they were patrolled, by both county sheriffs and city police.
And actually, this is my fourth campsite, I take that back. 'Cause one
of them I was given a notice that I had to leave from that area.*

   *So I moved up another mile and a half or so . . . It had a nice view of
the whole west side of the city, I could see really clear in the night when
the lights come on and everything. So that was really nice, I kind of felt
like, you know—hell—like people in Hollywood, you know, up in the
hills . . . But I had to move from there too.*

Kay and Samuel have a history in the town. It's where Samuel
grew up. This is one of the reasons why he feels he can live within
city limits in an area nearby one of the city parks. *"Don't tell anyone,"* he confides in a whisper, looking to see who is in earshot,
because we both know this is illegal. When the weather is really
bad, neighborhood people let them sleep more sheltered on their
property. But most of the time, Kay and Samuel (who have been
together for years) sleep unsheltered.

Part of keeping yourself and your possessions safe means distancing yourself from people who would cause trouble and invite attention and, ultimately, the police. This is why Kay and Samuel keep their eyes on the "street rats," as they call them.

"Who is that?" I ask.

"Like the people over there." They point to a group of four, seated in the corner of a pocket park only thirty feet away, who appear to have been drinking and whose conversation occasionally erupts into loud laughter or rowdy outbursts.

"Street rats," they repeat, *"drunks. If we see they're here, we move to the other part of town. The police know we're okay, but we don't want to get in trouble by being near them when something happens."*

Finding a spot is the first skill. But there are more skills—even what you would call expertise—needed to navigate a homeless life. The rest of this chapter relies on my encounters with people you have met—Randy, Ross, Jerald, Kay and Samuel, and Penelope—to demonstrate some of the know-how, resourcefulness, and resilience required to live homeless and unsheltered.

Protecting Your Stuff (and Yourself) 101

Most people think that the homeless don't have possessions, at least no possessions of value. Homeless people definitely don't see it that way, and one of the challenges they have is to protect their belongings from human and natural elements.

One of the first things Jerald had to learn was to withhold information:

Say somebody asks me where I'm camped, I wouldn't tell them where exactly I was at. "I'm just in this area here," I tell them. But I wouldn't give them exact locations. That way nobody would know where you are at, where you are located at. No one would be able to steal your stuff or anything like that. For my own safety [too] like I said I'm not going to tell you where I'm at. Or really what I'm doing.

To protect his campsite while he is at work, Jerald has learned to break down his camp every day so nothing appears to remain on the surface. He collapses his tent, then folds everything underneath, then covers it flat with a brown tarp.

Some other forest dwellers Jerald knows will pack everything up, bag it, and try to store it somewhere. But then they have to return all their belongings to the site each night, unpack everything, and set up their camp again. *"I don't see the sense in that,"* he commented, *"but some people do that too."*

"I try not to make it noticeable," he explains. *"So that way if people were to come by they're like, "Oh, it's just like somebody's old stuff or whatever. They just left it there." But what they don't know is that everything is all laid out . . . inside.*

"I've cut down several branches or whatever and use that as like a wall or whatever to keep people from seeing it . . . My tarp—it's brown. It's kind of beat up like a weathered rock. But everything, you know [important], its covered on the inside. It's camouflage," he says with some pride.

The most visible and vulnerable homeless wheel their possessions openly in a shopping cart, where they can monitor their stuff and keep it close. This is often what the public associates with homelessness, but most unsheltered people don't want to be visibly marked by a packed shopping cart. What's more, the supermarkets and malls are pushing back. Homeless people who want to navigate the landscape with a borrowed shopping cart are encountering new technology that embeds sensors into the carts so they won't move if taken off the property. In the shopping center where Randy keeps his car, new posted signs show a shopping cart at the edge of a bright yellow line with a red "prohibited" symbol through one wheel: They read: *"Attention Shoppers! Our shopping cars will lock if taken beyond the parking lot perimeter. While distinctive yellow lines mark normal exits, the entire lot perimeter is protected."* The same message then appears in Spanish.

When some cities went so far as to outlaw shopping carts outside of parking lots—another approach to the perceived problem—homeless started using baby carriages to transport their possessions.

And then there are storage units. It was Ross, and his gift to me of an original oil painting (see chapter 3), that made me begin to notice the prevalence of paid storage areas among the homeless. This (reconstructed) exchange, several years into our friendship, took place at a time when Ross had first moved into a subsidized motel and proffered his gift:

> *Cathy: It's beautiful . . . but where did that painting come from?*
>
> *Ross: A homeless Native American guy, an artist, gave it to me a couple of years ago for helping him out.*
>
> *Cathy: But where have you been keeping this?*
>
> *Ross: My storage unit.*
>
> *Cathy: You have a storage unit!?*

I thought Ross was an outlier. (What homeless person living unsheltered in a park or a forest would be paying rent for a storage unit?) But then the subject of storage units and why he wanted one came up spontaneously in my conversations with Jerald as well:

> *I try to keep what I have at camp to a minimum so I don't have too much there. Especially valuables and important stuff I know I shouldn't keep there. I try to keep those, you know, at a different place . . . I've been*

wanting to get a storage [unit] so I can store all my camp gear because I don't want to sell it, I may need it again. I don't want to get rid of it or anything. So that's another thing I'm looking into.

I began to realize that I never noticed or broached the topic because, in my own mental separation of homeless as a subculture, I missed the sameness, the "us-ness," that homeless individuals continue to hold close. The storage unit was a repository of that sameness, retaining possessions that evoked a better past or envisioned a brighter future; they stored items that were security and insurance, hope and dignity, an identity of being, really, just like everyone else.

It was not long before I came to see that there were *many* other homeless who had storage units that they paid for by the month. Some kept possessions there to sell or pawn for extra money, while others simply could not abandon valued property that was hard-won. Still others held on to objects and mementos that linked them to a happier past. Some stored items for the day when they would once again have a place to put them. Some lost all their possessions because they couldn't keep up storage payments and their unit contents were confiscated.

I was to find out, too, about the homeless people who lived in their units. For some, the storage unit became their day shelter, a place to go when they were forced out of the Community Shelter at 7 am on a sleeting winter day. I met shelter residents who had pooled their resources, earned partly through plasma donation (see chapter 6), to jointly rent a unit, where they stored their gear and socialized during the day. They returned to the shelter at night for warmth and food. For some, like Penelope, the storage unit truly was their residence.

When I first met Penelope, whom you encountered in the last chapter, she was staying in a shelter, but she had spent the past summer living in the storage unit where she kept her possessions. *"They didn't know,"* she added. She is not the only one with such a story.

This is less difficult to fathom when you realize that a fifteen-by-fifteen-foot (225 square foot) storage space runs about $135 to $155 per month in a town where, in the summer, a Motel 6 room of the same size, even at weekly rates, costs more than $1,500 for the month. The worst-rated motel in town, with black mold and stained towels, will run $325 a week. There are cheaper alternatives, but many are problematic, ironically, for those with little money. A single room for rent will probably run around $500 a month, but it typically requires a security deposit, or first and last months' rent—precisely what a poor and homeless person will not have. So the alternatives, besides the shelter, are unrealistic. Penelope told me:

> *What I do is, when I was going there, is wait until the storage people leave. They leave like at five thirty pm. So I'll go and wait until eight, some nights. So during that summer, I had this big old place to stay in there. I had all my covers in there, and my Internet.*

She explained to me how, with a little fiddling, she could open the door of her storage unit when she was inside it, how you could leave an unnoticed space underneath the door for more ventilation but leave the lock on, so it appeared closed. How the storage people didn't look closely, despite some cameras in the facility.

"The storage people come in," she told me, *"at eight am. So I'll get up early in the morning. Set my Android to alarm, so I'm gone. And maybe I take a shower at the storage."* (There was a bathroom.) *"I'm gone before they come to work."*

The Art of Keeping Clean

When you are living unsheltered, part of staying safe—from both the law and public scrutiny—is looking "normal," and part of looking normal is keeping clean. This is most challenging for those without a sheltered routine and resources. It takes time and planning, more than in conventional living, to arrange for self-care.

"*I haven't had a haircut in, like, the last . . . like about a month ago,*" Jerald tells me. "*I need to do that. Sometimes you do need to . . . at least, you know . . . I'm homeless but I don't have to look like shit.*" He goes on, without prompting:

> *You know, 'cause I've seen, I've seen men and women who've, who've just, who are just totally in the gutter and they just don't have anything really and they're, you know, either on something or just all liquored up that they don't even care sometimes what they look like. And I've seen it out of certain people, even people my age, and I start to wonder, "Damn, don't you guys ever feel bad for looking like that or being this way?" Because to me, I know that would really bother me.*

Jerald thinks his haircut will help him to "pass," as he often does. As he puts it, "*I've kind of gotten away with being at certain places or just hanging out here and there. Like most of the time it was just to recharge my phone or on my way to work or . . . killing time to go to work.*"

People find showers where they can. If the timing and transportation are right, one can shower at the shelter. Some people use the community recreation center, which can cost only $6.50 a day for a use pass (but it offers communal men's and women's showers with cubicles, and the rate applies only if you can show town residence). You can clean up and shave at a bathroom in the mall, if your appearance does not raise the antennas of mall police.

Penelope talked about her strategy for staying clean, a strategy that many homeless would find familiar. "*I've gotten really good at being homeless. I figure out all kinds of ways to cope and get through life. Like I can take a bath anywhere. And, really, I've taken a bath everywhere,*" she says with a mischievous smile.

"*Like where?*" I ask her, with some good-humored anticipation.

"*Like here,*" Penelope answers. (We are sitting at the Burger King—of chapter 4 repute—where I had bought her a coffee.)

"*Like . . . across the street at the Laundromat. The doctor's office all the time at [the clinic]. At the library. At McDonald's way on the other side of town. At Walmart, too.*"

"*So . . . How do you do that?*" I ask. "*How do you take a bath at these places?*"

"*It's like a 'birdbath,'*" she responds. ("Birdbath" is the jargon used by other homeless as well.) "*I get undressed and then I splash water, raising up a little toward the sink, and I've gotten really good at it. The only problem is when someone comes in. You have to time it right, and sometimes you can lock the door.*"

Randy regularly uses the gas station within walking distance from his car. You have to buy something, he tells me, but purchasing a pack of gum entitles you to a key to a private bathroom. The privacy is why many considered gas stations a prime bathing place. Randy shaves and bathes daily at the gas station before returning to his car. He does laundry at the mall Laundromat and keeps extra new shirts folded in the back of his car. He attributes his longevity at the mall to his tidy look, along with his clean, newer-model car.

As Penelope instructs, you have to be "*fast and neat, so that if you come again they won't remember you and try to stop you.*"

The Talent of Timing Your Day

Bathing is just one of the activities that make up a daily routine. Charging phones, checking mail, finding food, doing laundry, getting money all must be figured into the schedule. For people in legal trouble, it also includes checking in with probation officers, getting drug tests, doing community service, or taking required classes.

Despite the not infrequent characterization of the freedom of "houseless" life, there is much more routine that you might imagine. Ross said it plainly, comparing his homeless life of many years to his life in 2018, after he finally received HUD housing (see chapter 8): "*I was more run by the watch when I was homeless than now. No doubt about it. I had to be so much more time-conscious in the homeless life.*"

Then he explained why. "*Like when I was living in downtown San Diego, and not working, I'd get up at six* [when it got light and he became more visible], *and then I'd need to plan my day around when and where resources were available.*"

> *The first thing is food, and when you can get it. You're restricted about when you can eat. Because different agencies have different times that they serve, and if you're not there, you miss out. We all knew places and times—where you could get a free breakfast, and the couple of spots you can get showers.*
>
> *Then lunch, and you have the afternoon for getting money or job interviews or whatever. It could be a medical appointment, getting clothes, getting sleeping bags, getting that lined up.*

As Ross put it, "*You just become time-conscious . . . You have to plan your days so you can hit each one of these places you think you need at the right time.*" And this need to plan extends beyond daylight. As he advised, "*You want to be back by dark so you can set up and relax.*"

"*Why?*" I asked, still thinking of the lack of obligation in unsheltered living.

"*Well,*" Ross explained,

> *people start looking for camps and places to camp right around dusk. Like, if you have a little spot and you don't have it staked out—which means you're not there to protect it—by the time you get there, you might*

not have it any longer. [In the city] there's a smaller [number of] select areas to camp where you are discreet and not out in the public eye. In the forest . . . you can go anywhere.

Jerald's life in the forest, and his description of his day, is perfect testimony, too, to the often tight scheduling of homeless life. Remember that Jerald works. And he has the added legal mandates of classes, drug tests, and probation check-ins (many of which are done by phone).

"*Basically, it's all routine, I guess. It's all a daily routine,*" he tells me. Before heading to work, he bicycles to the mall "*to clean up really quick,*" and then he continues the eleven-mile bike trip to work. Jerald then works a six-hour or eight-hour shift, depending on how long his boss needs him.

There is no public transportation available when Jerald is finished with his shift. "*My bike has been my mode of transportation, that and the bus, but the buses don't run that early, you know, till about six thirty in the morning. So when I get off at four, or six, I bike all the way back to clear . . . clear on the other side of town.*"

When he wants to take a shower after work, Jerald stops first at the Community Shelter for the morning shower time. He charges his phone and heads back to camp for a little sleep before he has to get ready to go to work again at 6:30 pm. The mandatory classes Jerald must take add to the mix. Some nights, like on Mondays, he must fit in going to class *and* working. He comes home from work and goes directly back to camp for some sleep. Then he must turn around, get to the shelter to shower again, and get ready to go to class. "*I'm still tired,*" he shared, "*and I found that I fell asleep through class, this past class. I fell asleep in there, so I had to get up and walk around.*"

Randy's day is run according to his panhandling schedule. He gets up at 5 am every day so he can meet the early breakfast crowd at the McDonald's by 5:30, where he sets up in the parking lot. He moves to the shopping center in late morning to catch those shopping or eating out during their lunch hour. He favors the entrances of the shopping center again right after the workday ends. During the slow time in the afternoon he may do laundry or buy food. He gets $192 a month in "food stamp" funds, now called the Supplemental Nutrition Assistance Program, which appear on his debit card. Randy finds this stretches well, especially with the fast food gift cards or occasional boxed lunch from Chipotle, which some people give instead of cash. The SNAP food assistance program has been the subject of congressional debate about massive cuts, which could see his monthly allotment drop to $134.

When the car is running and movable, he tries to park it so its back window faces west, where the sun will travel in the afternoon. If he has cooked food from a handout or store, he will put it in the window. He calls it his "makeshift microwave," with a smile: *"It gets pretty hot in there [some times of the year] and if I leave food there a couple or three hours, at least I have a warm dinner. Maybe not hot, but warm, and it feels like cooked food."*

"It's a choice every day when I wake up," Randy tells me. *"To be happy or to be miserable. I try to stay happy because I'd rather be that, rather stay positive. Why not be happy?*

6

Making Money

For many homeless people, one of the tasks to be accomplished, usually each day, is to get money. This is easily a book in itself. How do homeless people get money? It may come as a surprise to many readers that a sizable proportion (45 percent by some accounts) of able-bodied homeless people get their money from working a job. Many I have met personally work seasonal jobs in construction, as agricultural workers, in fast food restaurants, as cleaning staff at local motels, as aides in elder care. This chapter explores the alternatives to working a regular salaried job, looking briefly at three moneymaking avenues—entrepreneurship, plasma donation, and panhandling—and then providing a more detailed account of one of the main avenues for the homeless to find work: day labor.

You have probably seen the sign "Will Work for Food" being held by some homeless person, typically at an intersection. Really? I have wondered myself, and the considered response I would give after many years of interviews may surprise you: probably *not* true. It is not because the homeless don't want to put in an honest day's work. Quite the contrary. It's that their needs and obligations go beyond food, which communities have become better at providing. Many of these other needs require money.

Among the first of these money needs is an avenue for communication, because homeless people, and particularly those who are unsheltered, are hard to find. Where can a government office like the Veterans Administration find you to tell you that your surgery has been approved? How can a probation officer verify that you are where you say you are? How can you be informed that you have received HUD housing? How can a family member find you to offer some help?

For those who don't qualify for free government phones with limited-use minutes (still called "Obama phones" by most), there are the regular monthly costs associated with basic cell phone service. The majority of homeless carry a cell. Many will also need money for a mailbox to receive official mail from government programs like Social Security. Your Social Security disability check might be reduced if you are living in a shelter and using its address, because the government takes out money for the shelter benefits provided. So many, even sheltered, homeless rent a post office or UPS box or, alternatively, often just an address provided for profit by a small business owner with a storefront.

It costs about $45 for six months' rental of a letter-size box at a post office. If you want to receive a package that will get held if it's too big for the box, then you will need to go to UPS. The cost goes up to $25 per month. For Randy, living in his car, it is worth it because, as he tells me, *"they don't throw things out."* If you need a place to hold valued belongings, then a storage box is needed. The smallest storage bins available in this area are five-by-five-foot boxes, which run about $50 per month. Although alcohol and drugs are certainly a focus for some in procuring cash, so too are bus passes, a shower at the local Y, food you have chosen rather than been handed, or even a motel room on a bitterly cold or stormy night.

If you are living in your car, you must stay legal and register the car. This is usually the biggest expense for a homeless person with a vehicle: car registration. Then there is gas, which allows you not only to travel for resources, such as a food box from the food bank, but also to move your car occasionally so it is not so noticeable.

The Entrepreneurial Spirit

Moneymaking among the homeless runs the gamut. Some people, like Kay and Samuel, whom you met when they were panhandling on a corner in the last chapter, also do odd jobs. Some are more entrepreneurial, either legally or illegally. Jerald used a borrowed toaster oven, burner, and microwave to cook and sell food—mostly to other homeless. He would buy raw food with his food stamps and intermittent earnings, and then prepare different items for sale. *"I even had my own sign for it. Drew it up,"* Jerald declared with some pride. Co-author Jason, who would sometimes purchase a breakfast or sandwich, said the business sign was lettered skillfully on a paper plate, and read "BIG BEAR GRILL." Jerald saw his cooking as both a business and a service that made him feel good:

> *I'm more about feeding the people and . . . I didn't charge very much; I mean, it was a very good-size portion and I didn't charge very much for it . . . Some of the people . . . all kept telling me, "God these are good." You know and so that's where the idea for the restaurant came up for all of that. So, at some point I do want to start something like that. And, like I said, I know I have the skills to do it and everything.*

His makeshift business ended when he found a regular wage job.

I have met others who will buy soda or beer in a six-pack or carton and then split the pack into single-can sales—again, often to other homeless—for a small monetary gain. Jason witnessed a free-market competition between two shelter dwellers who bought sodas with food stamps and then resold them for fifty cents each to other residents. Tidier profits were made by a group of homeless men, reported by Ross, who ran cigarette cartons (illegally, of course) from Mexico into California.

Illegal activities, though not stressed in this book, are certainly a part of homeless existence, often a product of the constraints preventing homeless people from finding legitimate work; other times, they are the collateral damage of addiction and dire poverty. Ross reflects that, over the years, most crimes he has witnessed or known about are committed by homeless against other homeless. As he shares with me, *"You get desperate enough, cold enough, hungry enough, and you can find yourself doing anything—becoming a person who you wouldn't recognize."*

Ross, Jason, and I have all seen examples: a shelter resident carefully watched by other residents because she meets her needs by stealing from them; a woman who parks her sleep-in car at a highway truck stop, where she turns tricks with drivers for her gas money and food; a couch surfer and part-time shelter resident who peddles "technology," a single cell phone or printer or tablet that everyone knows is stolen; a forest dweller who uses the public library computer to post ads on Craig's List for homosexual sex so he can get some income. There are shelter clients who sell their SNAP vouchers (aka food stamps) to others at a discount, a quid quo pro arranged as "I'll go with you and buy you $100 in groceries and you give me $50 cash." There are even more organized efforts of theft in which specific goods are stolen from local big box stores or supermarkets and resold, sometimes with advance customer orders. No one speaks proudly of what they do. It just is done.

Between the mid-1970s and 2004, whenever Ross wasn't work-ing for wages, one of his staple money-getting pursuits was collect-ing cans—the iconic homeless industry. He'd go to parks, picnic areas, Dumpsters, and other likely places. It was lucrative in San Diego and competitive. Ross did this up until he left the area in 2004. At the time, buyers paid $1.25 for a *pound* of aluminum, which amounted to either thirty-one tall cans or thirty-eight reg-ular-sized cans. On a good day you might collect ten pounds of aluminum (between three and four hundred cans that you could carry in a shopping cart) in a few hours to bring home $11.25. Most days, if he worked at it, Ross could make $20 to $30. In states where recycling has not been made a priority, like Arizona, the payoff is not enough to be worth the time, so you see few takers among the local homeless.

Plasma

The other avenue for earned income common to homeless people is selling plasma. The plasma industry would vehemently deny this and, in fact, aggressively discourages it. To be eligible for plasma donation, you must not have recent or excessive tat-toos, and be between eighteen and sixty-five, as well as pass blood screening tests for HIV and hepatitis. Legitimate donors, accord-ing to the industry, do not include anyone who cannot provide an address or who provides a shelter as an address. Still, when you talk privately to homeless people, you find that selling plasma remains a source of income for many.

You are paid usually by your weight, sometimes by your time, because that correlates with how much plasma your body can donate. In a procedure called "plassing," a technician inserts a nee-dle into the arm and extracts blood, and then uses a machine to separate the plasma from the blood cells, which are recirculated back to the donor. It takes about an hour and a half, after the initial longer intake visit, and donors receive cash payments on a debit card.

Most people make $30 to $40 a visit. And you can use the debit card cash immediately. What's more, the centers, historically, have been five to eight times more likely to be located in economically disadvantaged census tracts than they would be by chance. It is no surprise that the industry attracts the poor or that, as *The Atlantic* reported, "the number of centers in the United States ballooned during the Great Recession with 100 new centers opening . . . Total plasma donations almost doubled."

Before being diagnosed with diabetes, Ross donated plasma regularly over the course of three decades, often having his plasma drawn twice a week. The industry continues to thrive in the United States, according to researchers H. Luke Shaefer and Analidis Ochoa, "because the country allows compensation of donors (*many countries do not*) and has some of the least restrictive plasma regulations in the world." The U.S. Food and Drug Administration (FDA) allows two donations within a seven-day period, with at least forty-eight hours between donations. This adds up to being able to legally donate as many as 104 times a year, twice a week for fifty-two weeks, compared to forty-five times in much of Europe. Although many blogs and articles question the safety of ongoing twice-weekly donation, it is still within the law, and most plasma businesses use their marketing expertise to encourage you to donate regularly and often.

The handful of big plasma companies that dominate the U.S. industry offer special pricing and promotions to encourage this multiple and ongoing donation. These range from rewards programs, in which donors redeem participation points to earn e-gift cards and sweepstake prizes, to frequency bonuses (an extra $60 to $75 for donating twice a week), to status levels (bronze, silver, gold, and platinum) for which the rewards get better the more you donate, and to keep you active, your points lapse every thirty days. One company's strategy is to pay donors $20 for the first donation of the week and $40 for the second donation of the week.

The result is a highly lucrative industry, that has tripled in donations in the last decade, with more than six hundred donation centers now in the United States, and growing. U.S. donors supply 70 percent of the worldwide collection of plasma. It is a donor base that draws disproportionately on the pool of those who need ready money, from students and minimum wage workers to the unemployed and the homeless. A popular "homeless advice" website openly recommends, "One of the best ways to make money when you're struggling and homeless is by donating plasma." Ross agrees.

If your health status, or your needle-sticking tolerance, is not up to par, or you cannot find a way to come up with an address (of a relative, perhaps), this will not be a route to income. Often these are the same people: those with health issues, who find it difficult to work on a regular schedule. For them, and others too, panhandling is the answer.

Panhandling

In some countries, like India, begging is considered a legitimate job. In this country, begging is a source of shame, for many years even an illegal activity in certain places. It was only very recently, in fact, that laws criminalizing begging were challenged as unconstitutional.

To be sure, there are probably some professional panhandlers who are not homeless, and have cultivated a lucrative practice, and a spot during rush hour. This is the stuff of numerous articles, and is not surprising, then, why some middle-class people I speak with about homelessness echo this perception: "I hear they make more money than I make!"

But this is not generally what you find when you talk with someone panhandling (or, in the younger insider parlance, "flying a sign"). Published studies and experiments in panhandling put an average daily take in a large city location at about $25 to $30 per day. My experience with panhandlers in our smaller city would suggest a bit less; a very "good" day at a prime corner might solicit $30, but most "flying their signs" make much less. And many who make their living this way would not choose to do it. Three different panhandlers I've met used the same word in talking about their experience asking strangers for money: "humiliating."

Samuel, native to the town, and Kay don't panhandle in the neighborhood that "knows" them, where Samuel grew up. Perhaps it is because they find it embarrassing. Perhaps it is because they rely on people in the neighborhood for their occasional odd jobs: raking leaves, stacking wood, and doing other house and yard work for money. Otherwise they get their money begging on the street.

Samuel said he doesn't "own" a spot, but Kay said they *"kinda have dibs on certain spots."* One of them is on a low stone wall near a busy intersection with a stoplight—where I met them. One of the advantages here is that it has foot traffic as well as car traffic.

Between the pedestrians and the stopped cars, they hope to attract a few dollars with a sign, held by Kay, and written on a used, olive-oil-stained pizza box, which reads "Anything Helps. God Bless." The sign is tossed daily. When they have what they need for the day, they leave. If the spot is not good that day, they move to one of their other favorite locations. It is a schedule based on the whims of the weather, or if the local restaurant (where family members once worked) offers them food, or if "street rats" are near their spot.

Randy's days seem relatively more ordered. You met Randy in the last chapter, living in his car, with cancer. He panhandles on a daily route of a few blocks' radius that moves between a shopping center entrance, a McDonald's parking lot, and a Starbucks. He is not embarrassed by soliciting money, seeing it as a necessity of his circumstances. But when I asked him about what advice he'd have for me if I were doing this too, he told me to try my first couple of times panhandling with an experienced person because "*having someone experienced there, I think it's easier to take when people shout things at you.*"

Randy allowed me to sit with him many days as we talked. He sits in a folding lawn chair, wears a baseball cap that covers a full head of still brown hair, and holds a sign, on cardboard, that reads either "Please Help" or, on its flip side, "Kindness Goes a Long Way."

Randy works his spots every day. He is very clear about his needs and his finances. "*I need five dollars and sixty cents a day to live, along with my food stamps,*" he tells me. It pays for his car insurance, his gas, his toiletries. One of his criticisms of some other panhandlers is that they don't "*do the math*" but try to get everything they need in just one or two days. "*Like,*" he points out, "*that woman over there*" (another car-dweller we both know). "*She starts worrying about the car insurance the day before she has to pay it. You can't do that. You can't have to get all the money in one or two days. It's too much pressure.*

"*Me, I do the math,*" he explained. "*Maybe one day I make a little more, so I put the money aside because maybe the next day will not be so good. So if you're good at this, you don't try to get everything you need all at once. It's a mistake a lot of these guys make.*"

Randy understands his job as "sales." I don't mean this in a dishonest hustle kind of way. I mean it as understanding your customer. He explains that, when he first started panhandling, he would make a sign that said "Have Cancer, Please Help," but he found that he would make only $2 a day.

"*Why do you think?*" I asked him.

Randy responded after a moment:

> *Well, it's interesting. I don't think people really want to know the truth, you know, the details of why you need money. They just want to know that you are asking them for something, and that is why I've changed and I make my signs general. You know, 'Please Help.' They get it. If people want to give, they'll give; if they don't, they won't.*

Randy figures he makes $8 a day, on average, working three to four hours most days. Once, on a day during Christmas week, he made $50, the most ever for a day. He estimates that of every thirty to forty cars, one person gives him something, and by my reckoning, in the time I've sat near him observing, this is pretty accurate. "*Some days, if it's good,*" Randy explains, "*I stay out longer to get some extra for the days it will be less. It's not so good Monday to Thursday. My best days are Friday and Saturday. One day I remember I stood out there for three hours and got one nickel.*"

Randy likes returning to the same locations to sit:

> *You know, I have regulars that expect me to be at a particular place. I don't really know their names and things and they don't know mine, or my story, but I recognize them. One guy said, "Hey, you should know me. I've given to you four times before." Some people like to move around, but I like the same spot for that reason. People get to know who you are. They want to give something to you, not just to give. I think it's better.*

The Ins and Outs of Day Laboring

By far the most common way that homeless people earn cash is from paid work, and the most accessible way to get work is through "day labor" companies, usually referred to in the industry as temporary staffing agencies. The agency pays the day laborers for their work, while the business needing the labor pays the agency. The temp agency makes its money by asking more for its services than it pays out. The "markup" ranges according to the agency, as well as the specific contract it makes with a labor-seeking business, from about 25 percent to 60 percent. Agencies are quick to point out that they have costs they must pay, such as FICA, Medicare, and unemployment tax, but they also roll in expenditures such as background checks in computing their costs before they mark up.

So basically, if a laborer makes $10 an hour, a typical staffing agency charges the client company $14 or more, a fact not lost at all on the laborers. As Rick, a day laborer and shelter resident, comments:

> *The fact that they're making, you know, twelve dollars an hour and giving you eight. That's kind of a turnoff right there. Or they're making eighteen and giving you nine. You know, it seems like that's using people. And you know, people, especially people out here in the mission shelter, they just— they need a helping hand.*

So why do this? Why not just get a regular job? The remainder of this chapter answers some common questions, like this one, that a reader might have about day laborers, while offering a portrait of what it's like to be a day laborer. It is largely based on interviews and survey research conducted by co-author Jason Kordosky with twenty-four homeless day laborers, and it is informed by his own experience as a construction day laborer.

Why Be a Day Laborer?

It is not hard to understand why companies would want to outsource their labor needs through a staffing agency. They can try out workers,

hiring or firing with ease and impunity, simply by requesting—
or not requesting—that an individual return the next day. They can
expand or contract their workforce without consequence as workload demands. While they pay a substantial fee to the agency, they
are not locked into providing employee benefits, worker's compensation, pension plans, and other employee entitlements.

What is less easy to understand is why a worker would want to do
this. Talk to day laborers, though, and you begin to understand the
constraints that bind many homeless people who look for work.
Sometimes a worker simply has no choice. In certain industries,
companies have moved toward hiring entry-level workers *only*
through temp agencies, a reality that Billy, a homeless twenty-six-
year-old, confronted as a construction worker. *"I went to a couple
of the jobsites,"* he told Jason, *"and asked if they were hiring, but they
said they hire [only] through the labor place."*

Job possibilities outside of day labor are more difficult to find
without advanced education or skills, as Billy found out after putting in applications: *"Right now, it's pretty much the only jobs I could
get in town."* It is a common plight among homeless workers. Of
fifteen homeless day labor seekers Jason surveyed about their education, only one had a bachelor's degree; two others had attended
community college. One-third never finished high school, and
another third had a high school diploma as their most advanced
level of education. This is considerably less than for the average
American, limiting their permanent job options, but even this is
not the whole story; a lack of education is complicated by simply
being homeless, as Grace's story shows.

Grace vividly described what happened when her friend Adam,
a thirty-one-year-old living at the local shelter, applied for permanent work using the address and phone number of the shelter on
his job application. He got a callback for an interview:

"Hello, this is Community Shelter." (She mimics a shelter staff person answering.)

"I—I thought—" (Grace says stammering, now in the voice of the employer.)

"I was looking for an Adam ————."

"Oh, I'm sorry." (Grace switches to her shelter employee voice). *"We can't give out personal information."* (As a matter of policy, to protect the privacy of residents, the shelter will not reveal if someone is at the shelter or not, unless the caller is official.)

When Adam rushed back to follow up in person with the employer, the response was *"Oh, we already filled that position."* Grace continued:

> 'Cause he put in I don't know how many applications and they all did that. And I go, "Well, on the callback number, which number did you use?" And he said he used the shelter. And he thinks he got discriminated because he used the shelter address. And they're like, "Oh shoot, you know, this guy lives at the shelter. Are we sure we want to hire—?" And I think that was discrimination.

Grace is probably right about discrimination. And what if, on top of these other factors, you have rightly checked the box on most job applications that asks if you have been convicted of a felony? What are the chances that you will be the person who gets the permanent job? It is easy to see why so many homeless workers end up at a temp agency, apart from the positive advantages, such as being able to control your work schedule or decide the limit on how much you earn (see chapter 7). A past criminal record, a shelter address, and/or the lack of even a high school education make getting a job on your own a thin possibility.

Under these circumstances, temp work becomes the best route toward landing a "real job," and indeed, for the laborers we talked with, this was a key motivator. It is a belief that the staffing industry actively promotes. In Jason's surveys, the majority of homeless workers believed that the temp agency was their pathway to permanent work, but only a third had ever in their lifetime actually been hired permanently through temp labor. For most, day labor turned out to be a dead end rather than a steppingstone. Still, it offered a chance.

Other homeless workers turned to temp work because they needed cash in hand at the end of the day: to buy food for dinner, pay for a hotel room for the night, keep a cell phone operating, or manage the sixteen quarters it cost to wash and dry a load of clothes at the Laundromat. Without any savings or backup resources, many homeless workers—even those who would prefer permanent work—could not afford to wait the two weeks for a paycheck if they were hired in a salaried position. Workers who are homeless, then, find themselves in a position of having to endure the contradictions of temp work, in their words, *"the only thing available"* or a *"last choice,"* while at the same time it is *"my chance for a real job,"* *"a good way to make fast money,"* and sometimes the only legal route to *"same day pay."*

Getting There

You can better appreciate a day laborer's persistence and will to work if you have a sense of the hours before he or she shows up at the labor agency and stands in line, hoping to be picked for a job for the day.

Hopeful day laborers typically wake before dawn to begin their journey to the temp agency. Clyde would make his way late at night to sleep on a somewhat concealed park bench on the periphery of town, then awake and leave early in the morning for fear of being caught by homeowners in the area. Henry, only twenty, who came to town for work from a nearby reservation, would find spaces in the forest to pitch a tent. He showed the thick patch of trees where he planned on moving his tent so as to be better concealed from hikers. Neil, a sixty-one-year-old man who had worked in landscaping and ceramic production over the course of his life, also camped in the forest, sometimes with Henry. Grace, a twenty-nine-year-old woman, moved between this town and a neighboring city, sleeping near a park or sometimes at a friend's house. Adam also slept near a park on the edge of the forest.

Eric, who moved to town from Phoenix, typically found a different forest spot each night. The week before, though, he had missed the final day of his three-day job assignment because he overslept after bedding down in the forest for the night. So this week, before his reassignment interview, he picked a row of hedges adjacent to the temp agency in an effort to prevent another such misstep. He was not the only one to find a hidden spot near the temp agency. There was an advantage in arriving at the agency early, and sleeping next to it was one way to ensure this. Kelly slept in her vehicle, which she moved between parking lots whenever she was spotted and asked to leave. At the time of our interview, her vehicle was parked in the temp agency parking lot, where, in exchange for the parking space, she served as an informal steward of the lot by "picking up trash" and "keeping the drunks away." Matthew, who was fifty-five years old, also slept in his vehicle. More shelter than transportation, neither Matt's nor Kelly's vehicle was in any shape to be driven to a temp job. Billy, Levi, Oliver, Patrick, Rick, and Tim were all lucky enough to have a space in a local shelter.

When workers leave their sites early in the morning to head for the agency, it is well before the buses start running at 6 am, so most walk. It can be one to five miles from local shelters, often longer from the forest, as workers scramble down hillsides and trudge toward the agency door. Few job seekers stop for breakfast or a bagged lunch. Most are counting on the money they will earn today to purchase food. And so they make their way directly to the temp agency to be one of the first in line.

Waiting for Work

The process of getting work has just begun when a person arrives at a temp agency. When the door opens, the first in line signs in, takes a seat, and waits for work to be given out by an agency employee. Then the second. Then the third. Sometimes there are dozens in line. Most temp laborers subscribe to the belief that agencies do or should operate on a "first-come, first-served" basis in distributing job assignments and therefore arrive before the doors open in order to be near the front of the line. Then they sit, sometimes for hours, waiting for work. This is how Clyde described a day of day labor:

> *Usually, my regular—my day would consist of just waking up about four in the morning, you know. You know, wash up and be there by at least four thirty, four forty-five. Be [one of] the first couple in line just so they know that you are there to work. And I would probably wait for like at least a good hour to get sent out, between six and eight o'clock.* [It is only after all the traveling and waiting time that you then work eight hours.] *And, you know, a whole day would consist of a twelve-hour day. Just waking up at four and getting off at four and stuff like that. So, it's—yeah, it's a little stressful.*

The reality Clyde describes is typical. Temp laborers often wait hours just to get a work assignment, but they are not paid until they are on-site and their job officially begins. What's more, a laborer is never guaranteed work just because he or she has waited to be called or worked the day before, and may wait days or weeks in between assignments. Even when someone is picked for a daily assignment, there is no guarantee of a full eight hours of work.

Like Clyde, Oliver speaks of the "stress" he feels within this system *"when they don't call you out. Sometimes it will be a week. Sometimes it will be five days or less or even two weeks, you know. It's kind of hectic . . . Trying to figure out: How am I going to get some money? To pay your bills. Pay your phone bill or something."*

> Jason: *Do you ever know going in how long you will be working?*
>
> Oliver: *No, they don't let us know. It's just, you know . . . You'll be there thinking, "Oh, I'm going to get eight hours. I'll be okay. I'll pay my bill. I'll be all right." And then, boom. You only make about five, six hours, and they tell you you're done. Stressed out again and—you know.*

For temp laborers like Clyde, one's willingness to wait for work becomes a "performance" of sorts, an outward expression of one's motivation and interest in working. Many other workers described the purpose of waiting for work as Clyde did—as putting on a sort of "eager worker" show. For some it took the form of "strategic waiting": standing inside the agency—as opposed to outside, where they could sit—in order to be more visible to agency employees. As Oliver explained, it is important *"that they see you and get to know you"* because it tells the agency staff that *"this guy really wants to work."* Others would make small talk with employees at the desk. Still others simply showed up for days in a row. Rick explained why he went back to the same agency the second day after not receiving work the first. As another laborer had counseled him, *"[If] you go for two weeks straight every morning, you eventually get [sent] out."* The waiting time of "two weeks" kept being repeated in interviews with day laborers; through such prolonged waits, a worker could demonstrate his or her work ethic.

It takes its toll. As Oliver stated:

Yeah, it's kinda, you know, it's kinda hard. Struggling, like, you know, long days . . . You get your energy up, you know. You're going to get work, but you don't get nothing, you know. So you go to the next labor center right [over] there. You be sitting there waiting and you get nothing, so . . . Only thing is try tomorrow again.

On the Job: What's Different about Day Labor?

Workers fortunate enough to receive an assignment for the day were called up one by one by the agency employee and handed a "ticket," as everyone called it. The ticket told the worker whom they would be working for, when and where to show up, and a few words about the nature of the work (e.g., "construction debris cleanup"). It did not necessarily say anything about the length of the assignment or any additional jobsites the worker might be asked to go to during the day. The job might start right away, in a couple of hours, or much later for the occasional overnight shift. Some workers then had to continue to wait, unpaid, for their assignment to start, while others headed to their jobsite for the day. The assigned laborers would check out a shovel, push broom, hard hat, or any other equipment they needed for the day and leave the agency with their ticket in hand.

"Do you have steel-toed boots?" This was a typical question you'd be asked if you were working construction. Agency management required them, along with safety glasses or fluorescent vests for certain assignments. Because of the triangulated nature of day labor agreements, however, safety practices at work operated differently from other jobs. It was the temp agency that paid for workmen's

compensation and that had a financial vested interest in keeping workers injury-free. Yet it was at the worksites supervised by contracting businesses where the work took place. So although agency management required workers to wear specific protective or safety equipment for specific duties, they did not show up at the worksite to supervise and enforce their policies. And while the workplace regularly provided or paid for necessary equipment for their permanent workers, they did not do so for day workers. Therefore temp workers often had to borrow their safety equipment from the agency, leaving with the closest-fitting or least damaged item from the pool. On the jobsite, the worker often simply removed boots that were too large or a vest that was too small. Other workers successfully passed off their own shoes as steel-toed so they could wear shoes that fit.

Getting to the jobsite was completely up to the workers as they made their way on foot or by bike, bus, or car. Most workers walked, sometimes a few miles, to the jobsite carrying the equipment needed. Upon arrival, the worker would find the supervisor on-site (if one was to be found) or might otherwise call him or her on the phone to check in and get a better understanding of the job.

Job assignments varied from construction cleanup, "flagging" (i.e., directing cars through construction sites), or snow shoveling to janitorial work; from food preparation to manufacturing. The majority of assignments, however, had two common aspects: (1) they were physically demanding, and (2) they were usually "dirty."

Clyde talked repeatedly about the physically demanding nature of temp labor. He described digging trenches that required *"eight hours of shoveling," "carrying fifty-pound rocks,"* or *"pushing a wheelbarrow around all day."* It was all done, he added, working outdoors in the direct sun. Even for a strapping young male in his early twenties like Clyde, it was often too hard to work five days a week, every

week, at temp labor, and many times he would take a day off just to
"rest up." The physical demands of temp labor—"*hard work*"—was
the most universal refrain of homeless temp laborers.

At the same time, temp labor jobs were commonly "dirty."
Homeless workers frequently used adjectives such as "*gross*" or
"*nasty*" to describe their temp jobs. Although many dirty jobs are
done by permanent workers, too, dirt comes with a special burden
when you have temp worker status and you are homeless.

The worst temp job Walt ever had was at a food processing
factory, where "*they mix all the ingredients and stuff and it goes
through these extruders and stuff like that to mix it, and it's—you get
a lot of moisture, like water, in there and that's where you get really
dirty.*" He went on, "*It gets in your nose; it gets in your ears. It gets
everywhere and you stink like it and you're grossed out. Then you
have to change your clothes every day.*"

Regular employees get uniforms, but not temp workers. For Walt,
and other homeless temps who aren't provided with uniforms or
coveralls, they have the added tasks of finding a way to purchase,
clean, and store their clothing with no home or laundry facilities
and little money. And although the griminess can be problematic
for everyone who works a dirty job—temp or permanent—the
bigger issue for homeless workers is that their grubby clothes feed
the image of uncleanliness that is associated with being homeless.
Their conscientious work makes them look more noticeably and
stereotypically homeless.

Another confounding problem for working homeless people
has to do with food on the job. Marv, a forest dweller and temp
worker, described to Cathy his self-consciousness as fellow workers at the site broke open their lunch boxes for the half-hour lunch
break. With nothing to eat, his bigger concern was that no one
should notice he came without his own lunch.

Marv was more the rule than the exception. Few temp workers packed their lunch, as Jason observed, often because they either did not have the means to do so or could not afford to buy lunch until they received their first paycheck. Without lunch in hand or the money to buy food on the job, temp workers like Clyde were most likely simply to forgo eating during the entire working day. The problem led to a common strategy: temp laborers would arrange with their crew boss to work through lunch, with the advantage that they could then leave work early—giving them a chance to get back to the agency before it closed to receive a paycheck.

Three Don'ts: How to Be a Good Temp Worker

Temp workers labored for a daily paycheck, but they also worked to secure a "ticket" for the following day and, if all went well, an offer of a permanent position. This meant that each time they completed a day's work, they also enacted a performance designed to establish their good reputation and extend their work life. Such daily jobsite performances matter because client businesses are asked to grade the worker for the temp agency; they can initiate "return tickets" for workers (which ensure the workers a job the next day); and they have the ability to hire workers for more coveted permanent positions. To become known as a high-performing worker, improving the chance of a next-day hire and longer-term assignments, day laborers developed common strategies. Here are three of the most prevalent.

1. Don't be caught taking a break.   While breaks are a given in manual labor because of its demanding physical nature, some temp laborers indicated that they felt the need to work constantly; if they took a break and the supervisor showed up, it could appear as if they were not working at all.

Billy was one of these. His rule was: Always look like you are working. He was even uncomfortable when, during a legitimate lunch break, a fellow temp worker lay down on the ground to rest nearby him. Billy was afraid that it didn't look right; he decided to end lunch early and resume working because he worried the supervisor (if one showed up) might think he was lazy because of his proximity to the lounging temp worker. Many workers, including Jason when he worked day labor, felt a pressure to constantly work hard for fear of being caught in the middle of a break when the supervisor showed up.

2. Don't ask too many questions. "Clean up this area." This is the brief sort of instruction that a supervisor might give a new day laborer before walking off the site for hours. Workers more familiar with the site or the job might find the instructions transparent, but a new day laborer may not know the answer to many questions: Where do I put the debris I clear? Is lumber considered debris? Should metal be separated out from concrete? Should I put discarded trash in bags or in piles?

The advice that experienced day laborers offer is this: Don't ask. Asking too many questions on the job comes across as incompetence. Or you become known as bothersome. As a result, many day laborers don't float the questions they have. This often leaves them feeling unsure, hoping optimistically that what they're doing is right, or that at worst, guessing wrong will mean a simple correction from a roving supervisor rather than a call to the agency to withhold a return ticket.

3. Don't report injuries. Eleven of twelve workers who were asked if they were ever concerned for their safety on the job said "yes." Having an accident or injury could mean the temporary or permanent end of their working life, since most of the work offered was physically demanding labor, requiring an able body.

The majority of workers had never reported an injury during their temp work, despite the fact that temp workers are known to be injured at a higher rate than permanent employees.

For most temp workers, this was an area of uncertainty; they were unclear about what to report, and they were also nervous about the consequences of reporting. Nicholas, who had sustained a recent knee injury on his temp job, shared with Jason his worry about seeking treatment:

> *Nicholas: I heard that if you report you got injured or something they won't put you back to work. It's just a rumor, but that's why I won't go to Urgent Care, because I need more temp.*
>
> *Jason: 'Cause you're afraid that—you don't want—*
>
> *Nicholas: They'll take me off tickets. Won't send me out somewhere because I got hurt here. "How do we know* [he says as the voice of the agency] *you won't get hurt over here on this job?" Because I had a friend that did hurt himself working for them. They . . . quit sending him out on that many jobs.*

On the day Nicholas and Jason had this conversation, Nick was hiding his injury, but his swollen knee and its implications for his future work clearly preyed on his mind as he waited for his next ticket. *"And honestly,"* he remarked, *"I'm scared."*

If you look at their posted policies and materials, agencies would seem to press their workers to follow safety-reporting protocols along with job safety procedures. Some agencies displayed one-page documents concerning safety on the wall near the sign-in counter, and they encouraged the workers to sign a form confirming they had read the document before going out on a job. If you looked closer, however, agencies could convey a mixed message about safety and injury that increased the uncertainty for many workers. A wall inside one agency, for instance, displayed posters with safety instructions, depicting proper lifting techniques; posted alongside them were prominent warning messages about worker's compensation fraud.

It was not that workers were concerned about hiding a perpetrated fraud. It was rather that the warning messages had the effect of scaring and confusing them about reporting. Would claims of an injury or job-related illness be believed? If so, would they be thought of as irresponsible for getting injured or too damaged for hard work? Would they be branded as a "troublemaker"? Any of these possibilities might result in decreasing or shutting off their temp work options.

The uncertainty may explain why injuries or illness, when they did occur on the job (as they had with four of eighteen workers surveyed), often went unreported. Rick recounted one time when he had complained about becoming ill after he was sent through a temp service to a factory line:

> It was a machine shop, and you had to punch out these metal pieces for the car industry. They sent them to, like, all three of the big, big ones like Ford, Chevy, and Dodge. And, basically, you had this punch press thing and it came down "clunk-clunk-clunk" and it would go really fast.
>
> So, umm, it had this like antifreeze that was sprayed out from the side of the machine to keep the metal parts cold so they wouldn't actually get super-hot where you couldn't touch them. And the antifreeze would spray up and hit you in the face. So it would drip in your mouth. So you really got antifreeze in your face, in your eyes, and in your mouth. And antifreeze is really, really not good. And they did that. And they sent you from the temp service over to do that.
>
> . . . And I was feeling really ill from doing that like a month straight. And, uh, I said, "I can't do this." It cost me, you know. I mean I had to leave. And then of course once you leave a job, you quit. You gotta leave the temp service [too], 'cause they won't, they won't take you back.

Quincy sums up the advice on reporting injuries: *"You don't do those things. You know you are going to lose hours, so you don't say nothing."*

Pay and Promise

At the end of what was often a very long day that included getting to the agency, waiting for work, getting to the jobsite, and then doing eight hours of labor, temp workers would make their way back to the temp agency to collect their checks. If the assignment lasted longer than the temp agency was open, the worker would have to wait an additional day before receiving the check. There were mixed feelings about assignments that ran late. Most participants appreciated the extra hours because it meant more pay; but it could be hard to wait—even a day—for money already earned when immediate needs were so pressing.

The average pay for a daily job assignment among the people surveyed was $57, and a typical worker in the sample went to the agency five days a week and received about three days of work. Given these statistics, a temp worker would bring in $684 a month, about 20 percent of the average wage in the town and hardly enough to rent a room. The community shelter, in fact, is part of what makes the day labor business viable, a theme explored further in the final chapter.

Once they received their paychecks, workers would head to a nearby grocery store or other business to cash their checks for a fee (usually two or three dollars), then on to purchase food and find a place to relax, such as at the local library or shelter or bar (though only one worker mentioned the last). The final task was making their way to their respective spaces in the city or forest to sleep for the night.

A homeless worker would go through the same routine the next day. If he was singled out for a return ticket, he would work again at the same site, with a bit more familiarity and confidence. If this happened several days in a row, there might be that hope of a permanent job. Although Rick has never gotten permanent work from a temp job, he knows people who have. He describes how supervisors at the jobsite would dangle the possibility, a narrative that was repeated in different words by other workers:

> *Rick: After the first month I was there they were talking that way. "Oh, you're doing good. We might just bring you on and buy your contract from [the temp agency] and bring you onto permanent [work]." But yet it never, you know, never happened . . .*
>
> *It's not fair that they leave you the false impression that you're definitely going to get a permanent position out of it. Even though they know that you're not. But they are just kinda b.s.-ing you to work harder. And it's to come back to them. So that's another thing, basically, the lies that they feed ya.*

7

Navigating the Bureaucracy

It is not that Helen Walker wasn't professional and polite. *"Please come in, Mr. and Mrs. Moore,"* she says, as she leads the three of us to her office. She is seated behind her desk when she initiates the first conversation. She begins, *"I am conducting your interview for [this government office] today. If you're missing more than two things needed, I cannot complete the interview and I'm telling you this in advance."* Ross and Wendi are trying to qualify for subsidized housing.

It is courteous but *impersonal*, one of the six characteristics of a bureaucracy that the German philosopher and father of sociology Max Weber identified back in 1922. The impersonality of the modern bureaucracy was designed in service of fairness and impartiality, so that one's relationships or status, key movers in traditional systems, would not figure into the rights or services one has. It was intended to counter favoritism. Still, for me as a novice in the system that Ross found familiar, the initial lack of affect was startling.

It was only moments later when a second characteristic of bureaucracy surfaced: it is run according to written records. Ross has brought everything: their driver's licenses, their Social Security cards, their tax returns, their proof of address, their letters from all other bureaucracies (the VA, Medicare, SSI, food stamps).

"Are you legally married?" she asks.

"We are!" Ross exclaims, as if that is the best answer.

"Let me see your marriage license." And Ross produces it from the pile, dated 1989. More questions ensue, each calling for written documentation.

At least ten separate times a document is individually placed on the desk for Ross's and Wendi's signature and date. These either authorize the agency to access their personal data (income tax, credit history, medical records, criminal background), attest to something in writing *("I do not have any outstanding debt to any housing authority"),* or affirm that the interviewer has advised them of their rights and, mostly, obligations and responsibilities *("If you do not notify the office of any changes in your status in writing, you can be 'terminated' from the program").*

Helen sounds as if she were reading, but it is memorized: *"You must read and understand all notices sent from this office. If you do not understand, you may come to the office for explanation, but it is your responsibility to read and understand everything sent to you."*

"What address should material be sent?" she asks at the end. Ross gives an address that is not his residence, and questions follow: *"What address is this? Is this a post office box?"*

It is Wendi who responds, *"Yes. This is a mailbox at the FedEx building."*

Helen repeats, *"Is this what you want me to use?"*

Ross moves forward in his chair. Since he had just qualified for a VA program that offered temporary housing, why wasn't he using his address? Maybe it was that extra question, or perhaps the look on her face. He seemed to feel an explanation was necessary:

Sometimes I didn't know what my living circumstance would be and whether I would lose my [housing] and have to go to the forest, so we got

> *a post office box. Some friends say to me, "Why keep a box when you have
> a [residence]?"—but I say that I'm keeping it until I'm sure all the paper-
> work is through and that I am in the system for housing support. Only
> when I'm more sure and we're in our apartment will I let go of the postbox
> and change my address to my residence.*

This answer is satisfactory. Helen continues, *"You will be signing
some of these documents every year, and you must make sure that you
do this. We will need the sexual offender denial document, the statement of no debts with housing authority. your report of income . . ."*
she goes on.

The institutions may change. One agency deals with housing,
another with food allowances, still others with medical or legal
issues. The group may be government or private nonprofit. Some
may be a little worse or a little better in dealing with those who
use their services. But they share the features of a bureaucracy that
shape the experience of those within it. This chapter cannot detail
all the myriad agencies and their policies that homeless people
encounter, but it endeavors to show how our social institutions—
in addition to providing needed functions and services—help to
construct what it feels like to be homeless.

In the System

There can be no doubt you have entered a system. Although
this feeling is probably familiar to every reader who has been to a
motor vehicle bureau, if you are homeless and dependent on the
bureaucracy for resources, this is what most of life feels like. As
Weber predicted, bureaucracy can become a form of domination.

When I first saw the eighty-year old woman shuttled from the
regional hospital to a local shelter, she was sitting outside, waiting
to be assigned a bed. Her legs were horribly swollen from a recent

procedure, and the walker that she had been given at the hospital had plastic bags slung over each handle with medical supplies. She waited outside for a half hour before she was called in to get a bed assignment. As she trudged her way to the shelter door, with her bundles and bandages and medical supplies, the first thing I felt in myself was a sense of alarm. How is she going to make her bed? How will she be able to get a tray of food to eat when she needs her hands for the walker?

I was volunteering. *"Would it be okay,"* I asked gingerly of a staff member, *"if I made her bed?"* I would know the answer now, after being in the system for a while, but I did not expect it then. The answer was no. The people answering were decent, wonderful people. But we were contained in a bureaucracy that had to look impartial: All residents at the shelter must be able to fend for themselves. There is no special treatment, no rule that doesn't apply to everyone. It is really no different from the airport lounge that will not serve me a beer even though I am the same age as the server's grandmother until I dig through my luggage to find the ID I have already packed. *"I'm sorry,"* says the server, *"we have to card everyone, or I will lose my job."*

It is just another version of the impersonal, impartial way that bureaucracies run. It also illustrates a third feature of bureaucratic institutions: rules and regulations, which typically define and control the way that behavior takes place. *"But what will she do?"* I press quietly so that other shelter residents don't hear my protest about the octogenarian. *"She can ask another resident,"* I am told. *"Someone else can help her."* (The rule is that staff and volunteers cannot step in and do something that is expected of a resident.) And here too you can see another feature of bureaucracy: it is hierarchical. Each rung of the ladder has a specialized role, and they differ in power. The interactions between those on different rungs, even different levels of staff, from junior to senior, from clerks to supervisors to management, are strictly prescribed.

The language of these systems obscures the hierarchy that everyone knows to be the case, as if the terminology we apply to homeless could impute power or dignity or agency. In shelters, homeless people are "residents," the term you might hear applied, ironically, at a homeowners' association meeting. To social workers, they are "clients," what a corporation might name us if we had hired it or bought its products. When homeless sell their bodily fluids at for-profit plasma centers for needed ready cash, they are called "donors," the language of philanthropy. Day laborers are "contractual workers" or "freelancers," giving the impression of free choice and mutual agency that laborers really don't have.

Usually homeless individuals deal with the lower levels of the system, the clerks and staff and caseworkers with whom they directly interact. These personnel have their tiny domains of responsibility and power, but they can do little about the larger systems or policies that apply. They are what Michael Lipsky has called "street-level bureaucrats," the people on the front lines between the systems and their clients, who can interpret the rules or evaluate your case to tip it one way or the other. Typically overworked and understaffed, they often do not have the resources needed to meet the demands that confront them on a daily basis. To manage their unmanageable situations, they adopt coping practices whereby they ration resources, routinize interactions with clients, and screen out applicants who display unfavorable characteristics or uncooperative behavior. Ross has become an expert.

We spent an entire two-hour interview in which Ross gave advice about how to deal with "the system" and its agents. Here was his first rule: (1) *"You can't get the system to move any quicker than it does, so don't try."*

As Ross went on with his pointed advice, he sounded more and more as if he were the head caseworker at a social service agency. He continued with other bromides: (2) *"Keep all appointments and be on time!"* (3) *"Make sure all paperwork is completed from start to finish; correct information is what makes the world go round!"* (4) *"Don't wait until things become critical before seeking help. If you know that things are going bad and you're on a slow downhill skid, don't wait until you're on the streets in the middle of a snowstorm."* And, finally, (5) *"Even emergency assistance takes time, and it can be a real effort to keep your cool, but everything takes time."*

"Ultimately," he concluded, *"there are no surefire ways to beat homelessness, but you can minimize it and make it somewhat bearable just by simply jumping through the hoops as asked too. Do what they want and they'll do what you want."*

Ross was particularly skilled at "using one agency," as he put it, "against the other." What I came to see is that he intimately understood the workings of bureaucracy and how to parlay its hierarchy, its rules, and its paperwork, which today means a computer record, into resources. Look at how it works.

Ross was receiving a 20 percent disability payment from the VA. As his neuropathy and diabetes worsened, he was hoping to double his disability payment from the VA and also to apply for Social Security disability. He went first to Social Security. *"How can you prove that you are disabled?"* he was asked. *"Just check with the VA,"* he answered, where the computer records confirmed that he was already listed in the system as disabled. Social Security ruled in his favor. Then he returned to the VA for a jump to 40 percent disability. *"How can you prove your increased disability?"* was the predictable question. He referred the VA to Social Security, which was now paying him a full disability check. He's in the computer again. The VA raised his disability payment. He looked at me sheepishly. " *Well, I'm not making money off of it. I'm just getting what's right.*"

Many people do not end up getting "what's right." Even with a lawyer or advocate, your chances of being awarded Social Security disability benefits are only about one in three, plunging to 10 to 15 percent without an advocate. The main difference between those who are approved and those who are not often boils down to compliance. Those denied benefits were hard to contact, or had missed appointments, or lacked all the necessary documentation. As Matthew Marr, who studied homelessness in Los Angeles, concluded, "In the face of insatiable demand given limited resources, those who are able to meet these requirements are more likely to be deemed as cooperative and deserving and are awarded benefits." Alternatively, those deemed "uncooperative" don't get help.

Catch-22s and Favorite Lists

Even for those skilled in navigating the bureaucracy, there is something crazy-making about the structures that most homeless must inhabit. So much of one's life circumstances as a homeless person seeking help is a Catch-22, the term coined in Joseph Heller's classic 1961 novel to describe what bureaucracies do to people. Its formal definition is this: a dilemma or difficult circumstance from which there is no escape because of mutually conflicting or dependent conditions.

Catch-22 originally referred to an air force rule in World War II about who could be considered mentally unfit to fly, and therefore given relief from flying combat missions. The rule seemed to make sense: combat relief would go only to those who are evaluated by the squadron's flight surgeon and found not sane. But as the characters find out, you must put in a formal request to be evaluated as unfit, and any pilot who requests relief from flying dangerous missions has just given proof that he is quite sane. By the same logic, only those who don't request an evaluation might be insane, but they cannot be relieved of duty because they haven't put in a request. Get it? Of course we do, because it is the way so many of our modern bureaucracies work and how they ensnare and confound those within them.

"*I hate to say it,*" said Cal, who has been both homeless and an agency staff member, "*but you are better off being mentally ill in this system.*" He was talking about the ability to get resources. "*Having mental illness helps.*" His boss, who had been listening at the door, entered the room nodding. "*It seems a strange thing to say,*" she agreed, "*but in order to qualify for a lot of jobs programs, you need to be actively SMI,*" a term I had never heard of. It stands for "serious mental illness."

Jerald introduced the term on his own when he was talking about the great programs and giveaways one agency offered but he couldn't access. "*Yeah. Like I don't have a serious mental illness, like SMI or whatever, and I'm like, "Do I really have to be that messed up to be part of this program?"*" He continued:

> All the summer they've been providing people with camping gear. Tent, sleeping bag, tarps, water containers. So I've seen people go in there and walk out with that stuff and they've even taken people out to certain areas to camp [where I was] . . . But they say that since I don't have [an SMI] . . . I can only get so much help through them.

Jerald has been working for two years. He is sober, finishing probation, and striving to be proud of himself. As he told me, "*That's my thing is trying to prove to everybody else that 'hey, man, I'm still, I'm still me.' I can still show that I'm still doing something good. Not only for myself, but for to show everybody else out there. I'm doing something, I'm doing something good."* It is not hard to see how he would very much *not* want to be identified as SMI, but he couldn't get the help he needed without convincingly complaining of mental problems.

When Ross qualified for a new veterans' program that could subsidize his temporary housing, he moved out of the forest and into a "motel-by-the week" that he described at the time as more upscale—cleaner and with a better clientele—than the seedy, dangerous "welfare motels" he had known. I was excited for him, and it meant that Wendi could come and live with him. For the first time in a couple of years, they would have a decent room to call their own. Over time, though, all our enthusiasm faded.

Even with subsidies, and his new government benefits, the costs proved exorbitant, consuming *"every dime I make,"* he lamented. A few months into the venture, he shared that he was paying $267 a week,

> over a thousand [dollars] a month. The problem is because I'm paying what I'm paying and have other things to pay too—you obviously have to eat—it pretty well eats up everything, so I can't stockpile any money. I could rent a studio now, but with no savings . . . I can't deal with first and last month deposits, and deposits for gas and electric and all that, and so I'm stuck.

Plus, the rent changed every month at the motel, keeping his life unpredictable:

> [It changes] depending on the season. Even depending on what particular weekend it is. If it's a holiday weekend or something, the rates go [he lifts both hands to the sky]. So, as I say, it's precarious . . . We're basically living from paycheck to paycheck to paycheck, regardless of what we do. It's just the way it ends up.

Tim is a homeless worker who would like to get full-time work but feels he can't because it would jeopardize the government food stamps and health insurance he currently depends on. As a result, he is locked into the day labor system, where, despite the fact that he believes it exploits him, he can control the monthly income he receives. Here's how he put it:

> At a certain dollar amount, those [benefits] are cut off. So if I'm at a temp agency, well, "See ya later this month." I'm just not going to work anymore. It's based on a monthly deal . . . For example, there's two hundred dollars a month for food stamps and for health insurance [too]. So we are talking about four hundred dollars a month that would suddenly just evaporate if I took on their minimum wage job . . . It's just a very sensitive issue, but it's frustrating at times, as you might imagine.

Another Catch-22 really. The full-time but minimum wage job he wants would bring in more earnings than he has now, but his wage would be eaten up by food and insurance costs, leaving him with the same paltry income or less than he has now. No path leads to a better life.

The contradictions in the system ate at people. Day to day, most homeless people I encountered were surprisingly tolerant of the plethora of rules, the lines, the waiting, the monitoring, the paperwork, the constraints of space and time. It was as if the system was inevitable. The daily complaints focused on the few degrees that its agents—the staff, the clerk, the caseworker—could tilt it. Throughout my interviews, I was surprised at the number of times the issue of "favoritism" was raised, sometimes cast as personal, and seen within the larger issue of racism.

Some people we interviewed told stories of not being liked by some staffer, or contrary irking incidents in which personnel "played favorites." In Jason's interviews, Walt complained that the new girl at the temp agency was *"kind of blackballing me,"* limiting the job "tickets" he received.

Quincy felt pressure to cultivate employers' favor, believing that you'll get work *"if you start talking to them and being friendly with them. But if you just sit back and keep quiet, you ain't going nowhere."* Adam thinks there is a tacit "favorite list" at the agency,

> which I don't think is very right for the person that gets there at five o'clock. Wakes their ass up at five o'clock. Walks their ass down there—Oh, well, they have to wake up before five, like at four or whatever. Get down there. Wait in line. Put their name on the piece of paper and sit there for four or five hours while other people are getting jobs off of their favorite list.

There were stories like this at the shelter, too—a staff member or volunteer who "had it in for" them, a client who always got to stay late, another who never got corrected for the same thing they did—but I would hear it, again, about diverse people in charge, from parole officers to pawnbrokers to social workers. Unfair. Unequal.

I could see it in people's faces. It makes you crazy. Or it makes you angry. And if it is the latter, you'd better figure out how not to let it show. As a subordinate you must, as in all hierarchical systems, curry the favor of those in charge—or at least not curry their disfavor.

Don't get them mad. Don't call too much to ask where you are on the list. Don't act out or raise your voice if you're upset. Don't argue. Be respectful enough to sound compliant. Smile. Talk to them about their weekend. Jason called it a system of emotional control. Indeed, it is a system in which you don't just need to toe the line; you must look pleasant doing it.

The rest of this chapter is my fulfillment of a promise. I promised Jerald that I would say this. He proposes a challenge to those who work with homeless. Walk in their shoes. He wants people to see how it feels, to understand what it does to you. It is worth hearing in his own words.

Jerald: Take away, take away everything that they know and see if they pick themselves up from that. Just to understand how we feel.

See if they like to get hassled by law enforcement. "Why are you out here? How come you're doing this?" And see what kind of challenges they run into. 'Cause I don't—I mean like some of them, I wonder who is going to turn into a drug addict, I wonder who is going to turn to alcoholism.

Cathy: Do you think that would really happen?

Jerald: Yeah, there's almost a guarantee that something like that will happen. [It will] scare them knowing that, "I have to lose all of this [my place, my vehicle, all the things I own]."

Take all of that, strip 'em of all of that, impose all these things on them, stack this against them. You have this much time to get out. You have this much time you have to do all of this. Go try and find a job, try and find a place to stay. Try to get your own food, try to get your own clothing. Try to . . . you know all of that. You have to camp. You have to—You're subject to the same things we have to do. Go to these certain places. You're only allowed to go to these places unless you have this, unless you have that.

See, you take them out of their own element and put them into something that they're just not used to. How many of them would actually self-destruct? 'Cause I've seen—I've seen people that got stuck here and that had nothing to go on. I've seen them change into something that wasn't even them. I've seen them change into, you know, just being a totally different person. I know I did.

8

Home at Last

Or (the more accurate title): *Post-Homelessness and the Reality of Being Poor*

It was a couple of weeks after he moved in before I saw Ross's apartment for the first time. It was a bright studio, with a separate kitchenette and bathroom. A living room area was separated from the bedroom by a quarter wall, so that the bed, though visible, was partially hidden. A glass door from the living room opened onto a communal outdoor space with swings and play equipment for children. This was "home." Ross snickered when I asked him how he would describe moving into his own place. *"You know, the first time I saw the apartment, my very first thought was 'I wonder how long this will last.'"*

I was surprised by the décor, all recovered from a storage unit that somehow Ross had managed to keep. A huge Confederate flag covered one of the three walls with hanging space. It sat catty-corner to an equally huge American flag. In between, on the floor and on shelving stacked against the wall, was old—very old—stereo equipment: a reel-to-reel tape recorder, a CD player, an eight-track tape player with speakers, a record player, a pink and gray poster of a record cover reading *Pardon My Blooper!* (a comedy album of radio and TV gaffes which I traced to 1974).

On the floor against a second wall was an edifice of eight-track tapes and CDs and vinyl records, literally several feet high. Neatly stacked was an unlikely array of films, among them *Shaft, Civil War Battles, Jack and the Beanstalk, Airport 1975, The Nutcracker* (a Christmas concert), and *Girls Just Want to Have Fun*. The only other open spaces were hung with music posters, including a big poster of Janis Joplin. All seemed testimony to the last time in life (the mid-1970s) when Ross had disposable income.

If this were a Hollywood movie, the picture would end now. Homeless man makes good. Husband and wife reunite, grateful for new life and new home. More good news followed shortly. Approximately eight months after the move-in, Ross and Wendi made it to the top of the federal housing waitlist and received Section 8 approval to remain in their apartment with further subsidies that paid for 70 percent of their rent. Ross believes that his rise to the top of the housing list after years of waiting had to do with his inclusion in the veterans' program that initially got him the apartment. For the first time, Ross shared with me, *"I felt relieved."* He baked me a pecan pie.

Ross and Wendi's living situation was now more permanent, and the shape of day-to-day life took clearer form. The tiny living room space became more cluttered with shelving, plants, framed *Star Wars* collectibles that Wendi cherishes, and a small flat-screen TV to play old *M*A*S*H* tapes on the VCR. A few months into their residence, I saw that the Confederate flag had been removed. Ross told me why. An African American family lived in his building, with a little girl who sometimes came by to visit. *"I started to think it would make her feel uncomfortable,"* he explained, even though Ross's feeling toward the flag was more about being a rebel than a racist. Here was a good man. The floor and wall space filled up, and it was less than a year before Ross and Wendi began talking about moving up to a one bedroom, although their budget has not yet allowed it.

After an initial flurry of secondhand purchases to furnish their residence and settle into apartment life, their finances quickly became strained. One of the first things to go was the car, whose failing parts were costing more and more money to replace. There were vet bills for the dog. Then a string of medical incidents: Ross needed to have teeth pulled, then a hernia repaired. Wendi needed a hysterectomy, scheduled at a hospital hours away in Phoenix.

"How am I going to afford to get her back and forth comfortably, not in a bus?" Ross asks me. *"I'm thinking I can visit her every day and maybe stay at the Mission,"* a Phoenix shelter. Every day was more brainstorming and a new plan. I received a text: *"Here's a question for you. What do you know about setting up a 'go-fund me page' for medical-related expenses?"* In the end, a VA program helped with medical transportation, Ross pawned an item for extra monthly cash, I provided backup, and it worked out, despite weeks when Ross was in an almost constant state of worry.

From my observer perspective, one of the most important realizations I had about homelessness occurred just about a year *after* Ross was no longer homeless. One could see that life was certainly different—having an address and a place of your own where there was a kitchen and a bathroom and a bed, where you could hang things on the wall. But in certain ways, it was not *that* different.

What was most glaring was the overlap of being poor and being homeless. Both conditions are persistently plagued by little or variable disposable income. Both are immersed in an ongoing accounting and verification process with social, government, and legal agencies, and both depend on the same, often predatory businesses to conduct your life. To illuminate this, I invite the reader in the remainder of this chapter on three trips with Ross and/or

Wendi that I have been able to witness as well: a visit to a pawn-shop, a visit to a free food store, and a visit to a federal housing office.

In reflecting on the vignettes I selected for inclusion, I realized that I had never been to any of these places in the course of my own life. I had never pawned anything in a pawnshop (along with 93 percent of the U.S. population), nor taken out a title or payday loan, nor cashed my paycheck at a check cashing store. I had never visited a food bank except to drop off a donation. I had never been submerged in the line-waiting bureaucracies of government or social agencies to obtain my housing, my food, or my medical needs. It strikes me that in our increasingly income-divided world, we come to share fewer lived experiences and understandings, to know less of the quality and texture of one another's lives. It is from this perspective that these visits are offered. When taken together, they have much to say about the system that we all inhabit but that many of us know little about.

The Housing Office

Once a year, Ross and Wendi must be recertified to receive federal subsidies for their housing. Ross invites me to his 10:30 recertification appointment, and I am driving. *"Come early,"* he reminds me. *"I don't want to be late."* Ross is typically anxious about these interviews, because a change in housing rules or a missing piece of paperwork could mean a massive shift in their circumstances. Ross and Wendi qualified for a federal low-income housing program that seeks to keep rent at 30 percent of a family's income. Families still pay for items like utilities, but the government covers 70 percent of their rent for private but regulation-compliant units that meet federal payment standards for rental cost. By 2016, 2,217,000 households benefited from HUD's housing choice voucher program.

The city housing authority, which administers the program, is housed in a one-story sage-green wooden building that doesn't look like a federal building. Ross has been here before, first to apply for the program and once before now to get recertified. We enter the office, a small space with ten chairs lining two walls of the room. A teller-type open window, behind which stands a woman, is positioned on our left, revealing a phone, computer, and desk area. *"Thank you for showing up early,"* she says. Her space opens into the back, where there are offices. In the waiting area, besides the front door leading outside, there is another door—locked—that goes to the offices as well. Only a staff member can open it, and, as in a doctor's office, someone comes out and calls your name when it is your turn. As we sit and wait, a woman with her disabled son, an elderly man and his daughter, and a single man walk in and request to see someone. They are all told it will be several hours if they want to wait—the staff are booked with appointments—but no one stays.

On one wall of the waiting room hangs a large cork bulletin board with paper notices haphazardly push-pinned in: the hours of "The Cupboard," a new local food bank; a chart specifying the upper limits that HUD will pay for rental units; the details of a school lunch program; and various other rules and services.

A small flat-screen TV mounted to one wall facing our chairs flashes messages as we wait. Some are about the city housing authority and the available units: what you need to do to qualify; where to get and where to send an application; pictures of different housing complexes—one for low income, one for disabled.

Another message appears. It is about Ross and Wendi's housing voucher program. My eyes focus in. You can apply, the screen tells you and offers a website, but with a large-print caveat that there is an eighteen-month wait before new people can get into the program. The website, which I access on my phone, puts the wait at eighteen to thirty-six months, but this statement is printed below the wait time notice:

> The Section 8 wait list is currently closed as of October 10, 2017, at 11:30 am.

Uh-oh, I think. I hope this isn't one of the programs in funding trouble, and I'm glad that Ross and Wendi aren't attending to the screen.

The LCD screen flashes strangely juxtaposed messages. "Soak up the Sun," reads one digital headline, advertising free wildlife hikes. Appearing next is a text-heavy PowerPoint screenshot advertising the VA outreach support program; the next screen, more cartoon-like, reads "Things to Know about Bedbugs."

Finally, the door opens. "*Moore family!*" the woman says, and we are ushered into a small office we have all been in before. Helen Walker (you met her in chapter 7), the housing agent who conducted their initial federal housing interview, greets us. Ross sits with his stacks of paperwork as Helen turns to click-click at her computer. Ross and Wendi are "in the system," which means that Helen can access their income tax returns, their food stamp allowance, their VA benefits. She prints out something.

She hands Ross the usual papers to verify and sign. Yes, the paper generated by the computer from their income tax return is their real income. Yes, they acknowledge that they live in an apartment built before 1980 that may have leaded paint and they assume the risk. Yes, their apartment is a drug-free space. This must be signed and answered "yes" even though Arizona allows for medical marijuana, which Ross says would greatly help his diabetic nerve pain and for which he qualifies. Still, he cannot use medical marijuana without losing his housing, because the federal government does not recognize this as legal.

Helen looks at her computer. She tells them their food stamp income is going down from $249 a month to $245.

"*Why?*" Ross asks. She doesn't know. The only big surprise in the exchange goes the other way when Ross tells Helen about the upcoming change in his rent. The staff at the apartment complex staff told him that his monthly rent is going up $70. "*What??*" she exclaims. "*I have no notice of this! Well . . . they can't do that without sixty days' notice. And it needs to be in writing!*"

Her dismay clearly arises from her concern for the tenants—not just the lack of timely written notice but the reality that apartment rents are pricing many people, like Ross and Wendi, out of the market and forcing her agency to drop their apartment complex as a housing option. "*We stopped sending people to place there,*" she tells us. "*We aren't keeping it as a recommended or supported complex anymore for new people because they keep raising the rates.*" Despite the fact that the payment standard for the town (the average local rent times 1.25) has gone up from $844 for two people to $938 for the coming year, Ross's new rent will not be within that standard.

"*How many places do you have left that you can rent at the payment standard?*" I ask Helen.

"*Not that many,*" she says wryly, without providing the number.

The upshot is that Ross and Wendi can continue to live in their apartment, but the subsidy will no longer cover 70 percent of their rent, as the program intends. Ross and Wendi are responsible for the additional rental cost out of pocket. Ross seems to know this already. "*It's terrible,*" Helen adds. An increasing number of her clients, she says, must pay $100 to $150 a month of their own very limited income to stay in their apartments.

"So, what happens," I ask, *"if the apartment complex charges Ross seventy dollars more after proper notification, and he doesn't want to do that? Can he go somewhere else?"*

"Sure," Helen responds cheerfully. *"He doesn't need to stay in that place."*

"So . . . let's say that were to happen now," I continue. *"Could you find him a place?"*

She smiles a smile of resigned acknowledgment. *"Well . . . that's it. I've got twenty people right now searching and no place for them. That's the problem."*

The Food Cupboard

"The Cupboard" is the newest addition to our town's nonprofit food kitchens or services, open for only six months. In that time its business has tripled. It embraces a number of forward-thinking ideals, designed to address specific needs in the community: schedule most open hours outside of the workday; allow people to choose the food they want; don't require formal documentation of need. Begun by local citizens, The Cupboard is an innovative non-government-funded "store" of sorts, where individuals and families can come to choose food from shelves and refrigerated units.

It is a chilly November day with a light drizzle falling when we arrive. It is just after The Cupboard opens at 3 pm, and there is already a line of people at the door. The sign at the entrance discourages college students from using the service. "We have limited resources," it begins, and directs students to other agencies.

The Cupboard is open, but we stand outside waiting for people to leave. As one individual or family exits, another can enter. Only five households (even if the household is just one individual) are allowed in the store at a time. People stand in line huddled, their arms wrapped tightly around them, shifting their feet for warmth, but there is no audible complaining. The door opens and closes, letting one group out and one group in. After this happens five times, one more family leaves and it is our turn.

Inside is a sign-in counter where you must either show a card from a former registration at The Cupboard or register now. We are registering, and there is a questionnaire that must be filled out. Name, address, monthly income, rent, how many in the household. A volunteer staff member peruses the questionnaire and asks, "*What is your income from?*" Ross responds, "*Disability SSI.*" And she nods, as if to acknowledge that he should be here. What makes The Cupboard different from other service providers we have visited over the years is that no one asks for ID; no verification is required.

What makes it the same is that you are clearly in a system rather than the customer of a business. A big white board sign as you enter reads "15-pound limit. One milk, one meat only." There is a sense of oversight and control as you walk through the three aisles in the 1,200-square-foot space to choose items. On the painted shelves are stacked canned vegetables and beans, mayonnaise, jars of pickles, salad dressing, and boxes of stuffing. There are rolls, English muffins, loaves of bread, bagels. There is one jar of Nutella on the shelf but several of peanut butter, one choice of boxed cereal (Chex) that contains too much sugar for Wendi and Ross, and a small stack of tuna cans with a handwritten sign that says "2 only." The canned chicken stack has no sign, but there are only three cans there. We take one.

Against the back wall there is toilet paper, and a few small boxes of soap, toothpaste, and toothbrushes. On the side wall are four refrigerated units. One is taped shut ("Do Not Open"). One, which houses bagged salads and greens and frozen fruit, has just a couple of bags remaining. Another section is labeled "Dairy"; in it is a yogurt-like offering in small custard cups, and half gallons of milk. We grab a container of milk. An attendant (one of three in the public part of the store, probably all volunteers) stops us, waving us over to a scale: *"You have to weigh before you continue shopping."* This is so we don't go over our weight limit of fifteen pounds and need to go back and return items. We are two and a half pounds over. *"You have to take something out,"* she says. As we discuss what should go, the attendant assists: *"That milk weighs four pounds,"* she coaches. It is an easy call. We return the milk, leaving our bundles a pound and a half *under* the prescribed weight, and head to the meat refrigerator.

As we move to open the meat freezer, a different attendant— a man who coordinates the checkout process at the front of the store—calls out loudly, *"You cannot open that yet!"* We turn to look at him, and he instructs, *"You must weigh in."*

"We just weighed," I call back. *"We're still underweight,"* I say, thinking this will reassure him.

"No," he counters sharply, to my surprise. *"I am the final say. The weight here is what counts,"* pointing to his scale.

Ross could see I was rolling my eyes and quickly took over the exchange. *"Just listen to the man,"* I heard him say in a manner meant to be public as he lifted all the bags onto the official weigher's scale. I felt slightly embarrassed, reminded that I am very used to operating from a more assertive, privileged status.

The final weigher now places all our items in one box for the scale's reckoning. It shows that we are below fourteen pounds, the upper threshold allowed for final access to the meat selection. Now satisfied, he announces, *"Okay, you can go to the meat freezer,"* and we are permitted to open the door. Inside is a limited selection of frozen meat. (All probably exceed a pound, but for weighing purposes they are counted as only one pound each. I get it now.) There are tubes—"chubs," they call them—of chopped meat, packages of quartered chicken, and shrink-wrapped portions of beef, containing two steaks each.

Wendi grabs the chicken. She adds it to our box, and we try to move quickly to the door so the next group can enter. As we leave, a household with two members is allowed in the door.

The Pawnshop

Ross and Wendi agree that they have probably pawned the heavy fourteen-karat gold ring with diamond chips, left to Wendi by her grandmother, a dozen times. The last time was when Ross had a bad tooth and had to pay for a dentist. Another time they remember is when they were living in a motel and couldn't come up with their total rent payment. When Ross's car had a transmission problem, the ring was pawned to pay for the repair.

The ring is the most expensive single item they own that is pawnable for a chunk of cash; they last pawned it, they tell me, in October for $225. In December, when Wendi and I are going again to the pawnshop, it is not to retrieve the ring by paying off the pawn loan. It is, rather, to pay the interest on their loan so the pawnshop won't sell the ring.

This is really how pawnshops make their money. Their profits do not come substantially from selling items that people pawn but fail to retrieve. The pawnshop clerk tells me that most of the items they hold, including Wendi's ring, do not easily sell if they are "abandoned" by the owner. If she should fail to pay, his shop would have the ring melted down and sell the 6.4 grams of gold to a gold dealer at the going rate. (On this day in 2017, the price of a gram of gold is $41.45, which would give the shop $265 for the ring.) This is not what the pawnbroker wants.

Neither does the pawnshop earn its income primarily from interest paid by people retrieving their item after the initial loan is due. Ross and Wendi's $225 loan is, by law, limited to three months, at which time they must pay $316.25 to get their ring back. The pawnshop makes $88.25 in profit (plus a $3.00 ring storage charge), which might seem substantial enough at 39 percent of the loan amount.

The biggest contributions to pawnshop margins, however, are made by people like Ross and Wendi, who desperately do not want to lose their pawned item but cannot afford to retrieve it by the date when the loan expires. What they do is pay *only* the interest of $88.25. This ensures that the pawnshop will not sell their item. A new three-month loan is automatically reissued, and in three months they will owe another $88.25. When the next loan comes due, the borrowers may repeat the process if they cannot come up with the total owed.

If they do this for one year, re-pawning four times, they will have paid an annual interest rate of 159 percent plus the "ring storage fees." In one year, the $225 pawn loan will have cost them a whopping $353 ($88.25 x 4), *and* the pawnshop will still have the ring!

It took me a lot of figuring to realize that the transaction which Wendi was about to complete was an even worse deal than that—and it was not due to the intent of the pawnshop.

The young man behind the counter was attentive and caring as he examined the pawn slip. *"You have another month, you know,"* he pointed out. *"You don't need to pay the interest now."* Wendi had come in with a wad of bills in her hand to cover the interest on their loan (which must be paid in cash). *"My husband,"* she repeated to the clerk, *"just wants me to pay it now."* Ross wanted to pay the interest early, as I find out from a later conversation, because he can be sure that he will have the money only at the beginning of the month, when his SSI check arrives. He is afraid that if he waits until the thirty-first, when the loan is due, there will be no money left and he will lose the ring. *"She'll kill me,"* he said with a laugh in front of Wendi before we left. *"No,"* Wendi countered, *"my grandmother will come back from the grave and kill us both if I lose that ring."*

The clerk does Wendi's bidding. He takes her payment of almost $65 to cover the interest on two months of the loan. He then issues a new three-month loan—the policy whenever you pay interest owed—and charges the same interest rate. The problem with Ross's good intention of paying interest earlier than the due date is that it automatically starts this new loan. The pawnshops have fixed the math to protect their profits. The interest is heavily front-loaded, so it is in the first month of the loan that most of the interest is charged. If you retrieve your item early—say, a month after you take out a loan—you pay three-quarters of the total interest, in effect penalizing the early payoff. The last two months cost little in interest. So if you keep paying off and renewing the loan every two months, the annual interest charges soar, beyond even the standard interest rate, to 172 percent. To recover their ring at the end of a year will cost Ross and Wendi $613.15 for a loan of $225. Yikes! (Refer to the endnote if you want to follow the math on this.)

And even if the loan were renewed in the most cost-effective way, at the usual annual rate of 159 percent, many pawn clients would end up paying for their rings or power tools or smartphones many times over. This is because the typical transaction is not just one three-month loan; it is a cycle in which a client pawns, re-pawns, and redeems (85 percent of clients get their item back), only to pawn the same item again in a few more months when the next financial need arises. It is this pawn-and-redeem revolving door that pawnbrokers rely on for their livelihood, as the National Pawnbrokers Association's website makes clear. In its financial planning advice to pawnshop owners, the association notes:

> During the first quarter (January 15 to March 30), you'll experience a decrease in your pawn receivables as your pawn clients receive their tax refund checks and begin redeeming their merchandise. This subsequently increases your cash flow. Beginning April 1, you will see the same items that they redeemed returning to your pawnshop for a loan as well as what they purchased with that refund. This will decrease your cash flow, and it's important to budget for the increase in lending.
>
> The main focus should be growing your loan balance. As long as that balance grows, your interest payments, purchases, and sales will also grow. The loan balance is the key. Keep that component "well-fed," and your company will quickly grow.

"Why are you doing this?" I ask Ross when we return to the apartment. He answers back loudly, *"Because it's the only way I can get credit!"*

It is important to be a witness. The three visits recounted in this chapter are just everyday occurrences, not the stuff of high drama. But for me, they are telling. What they tell me is that the line between being homeless and simply being poor is thin at best, maybe even imaginary, because, like Ross and Wendi, people go back and forth between the categories. They show me that "living poor" shares the same qualities of vulnerability, uncertainty, and looming authority that shape the lives of the homeless.

Readers may see different truths in these vignettes of post-homeless life than I do or Ross does, but still, it is important for our empathy and our insight for us to have contact with these places and people that appear only dimly in our experience, or perhaps escape our view altogether.

"Would you read something for me?" I asked Ross, handing him my printed accounts of the three trips described in this chapter. He sequestered himself in my car while he read slowly through the narratives. I heard the door open as he emerged with pages in hand to join me on a bench. *"Okay, what do you want to know?"* he said without comment.

I was a little nervous about asking the question, mindful of how difficult mirrors can be. *"What do you see when you read these stories? What do you think they show?"*

Ross was silent for a while, reflecting. Then a slow pronouncement: *"Well . . . I see . . . I see it's a complete Catch-22."* His cadence gained momentum as he talked about his feelings of running around in circles, being on a treadmill, at how "embedded" the government was in his and Wendi's daily lives.

"How do you think these stories in your lives would be different if you were back being homeless?" I queried again.

The answer this time came more quickly: *"They wouldn't be different. Take the homelessness out of the equation—like, I mean, the forest, and a tent—the stories are the same. I have the exact same problems.*

"Don't get me wrong," he cautioned. *"What we have now sure beats out our prior situation. I am grateful."* In fact, Ross has said to me on more than one occasion that he feels as if he could be "the poster boy" for the veterans' program that got him into his apartment. *"But,"* he continued,

*Wendi and I talk all the time about how close we are to being homeless
again. It goes together hand in hand, poor and homeless. I need to go to
agencies for everything—for medical help, for food. The difference is that
I'm not living in a tent. [But] I cannot afford to go to the mall. I don't have
a car, and I'm glad not to have the car so I don't need to keep paying for it to
be fixed. I don't get the food I want—certain kinds of food—upper grades
of meat, name brand food. I can't buy it. Right now, whenever I have cash
I stockpile little items of value* [he is talking about his *Star Wars* prints
and cards] *that I can sell outright if I need to so the pawnshop isn't my
only option.*

It sometimes grabs me when Ross talks, my disappointment that
the long road from homelessness has not held more promise and
ease for my friend. Ross deals with the disappointment too, but he
turns it on its head:

*I think I don't suffer as much as some people in my situation because
I expect the worst. Then I'm not so disappointed, because anything
better is a plus. Every time I go to the mailbox, I expect that—there's
gonna be some change in some program I'm in. I get two letters a
month—it'll be from the Section 8, VA or DES or Social Security—
and I think, "What now? What's going to change now?"*
    *I do well because I try to expect that something will screw up.
Something will change. It's started to be that, if I don't get a letter,
I start to worry that I'm lost in the system or something really major
is about to happen.*

In the next and final chapter, we examine some of the larger factors that make this uncertainty so.

9

Blind and Delusional

It has been more than a decade since Ross and I met. He has gone from a homeless camper who lived with his dog in the woods to a partially disabled veteran in a subsidized motel to the renter of a HUD-sponsored apartment where he lives with his wife. In my relationship with Ross, I have gone from a wary stranger to a curious acquaintance to a real friend.

My friendship with Ross pulled me into a world I never expected to frequent. Our relationship has moved me in the minor ways we change. I make bags for homeless people I might meet—with snacks and socks and toothpaste—which I keep in my car and always have on hand. I perceive differently every parking lot I enter because I now recognize the vehicles that are residences. I volunteer at least one day a week at our local shelter. I find that I know many local homeless people now, walking with their backpacks, sitting at the curb, or even panhandling on a corner. Oh, that's Emmet. There's Miriam.

It's a profoundly different feeling. It is that felt connection that probably has caused the most disruption in my worldview. As with all other worlds I have entered, from a South Pacific island to a college dormitory, they have taught me about my own grounding in ways that I hadn't imagined and, often, triggered a transformation of thought and heart.

I now think that to say homeless people are invisible and misunderstood is misleading—not because it is untrue, but because it misses the whole truth. What it fails to recognize is the relationship involved here, the actor in this who goes unnoticed. Who are the homeless invisible to or misunderstood by? That actor is me, the reader, us, the American public.

The truth can rightly be said in another way in order to emphasize what is always left out. I would put it like this: When it comes to homeless people, the American public is blind and delusional. It is our relationship to the homeless that renders them invisible and misunderstood. It is always this half of the dyad that is forgotten: the perceiver, not the perceived. So this final chapter about homelessness is really about us.

There is no need here to ignite the flames of political arguments concerning the homeless. There are realities to bolster any ideology. You can see the folly of government giveaway rules that act as disincentives or the individual foibles that lead to a slide into homelessness. You can also see clearly the ways that homeless are caught in the Catch-22s of the system, how the status of homeless demeans and dehumanizes, and limits the potential for change.

I do not offer solutions to homelessness. Instead I ask: What can we do about ourselves? It is an inquiry that, I hope, will also bear fruit in the form of better solutions as our self-inquiry, and perhaps collaboration with the homeless, too, open windows of clarity and compassion.

In the Web of Homelessness

If you see homelessness as an aberration in our economic system rather than its product, then you don't notice what homelessness connects to, its interrelationships. Homelessness will appear as a special case, a thing apart, a subculture unto itself rather than a strand within the web of conditions of which we all are a part. Not only do the homeless and their predicaments become less visible, but so too do the forces that cause homelessness to rise or fall, the industries that service homeless, or the programs that affect the quality and tenor of homeless lives. It is hard to feel ownership over what is considered not in your world.

Understand just something of the slippery slope that allows people to slide into homelessness, and your attention will be drawn more to what causes the steepness and slipperiness of the slope than to questions about individual balancing ability, or the footwear that sliding individuals are wearing. There are larger issues here.

In conversations with service providers, I asked, what is the one factor that would make the most difference in your own work with the homeless? The most consistent answer I received was echoed by Cal, who works to transition people out of homelessness, in a formal interview. He worded it, concisely, this way: *"a supply of appropriate housing."* He meant housing with the right facilities (number of rooms, handicapped access, etc.) for the individual or family in need and also a residence that the person or family, with subsidies, could afford. It is clear from the preceding chapter that such residences are becoming fewer and farther between, and even government vouchers cannot close the gap between what people have in income and what they must pay in rent. When I asked homeless people the same question about the one thing that would make a difference, it was Randy's answer that reflected the response of the majority: *"a decent place to rent I can afford."* It is the same answer, really: affordable housing.

"Affordable housing" itself is not really a factor as much as it is a relationship. Housing becomes unaffordable because the wages people earn are too low for them to be able to pay the rent being charged. The questions then become: Why are wages so low? Why are rents so high?

The *Harvard Business Review* reports that the median hourly wage has remained stagnant since the 1970s, increasing just 0.2% per year, accounting for inflation, and offers two important pieces of information about why wages have not grown. The first is that companies are distributing less of their income to workers, from 65 percent in the mid-1970s to 57 percent in 2017. The second is that the income going to labor is being distributed unequally, or as the authors write, "The large wage gains have accrued to workers at the top of the distribution, and wages have been declining or stagnant for the bottom half of the income distribution."

These developments track predictably with the overall trend in the United States toward increasing income inequality. It can seem baffling that, in a democratic system that loudly and proudly proclaims a commitment to equality, over time, things have grown more unequal by every single measure of income disparity.

The U.S. Census reported that in 1977, the lowest economic fifth of the population in household income held 4.2 percent of all income, while the holdings of the highest fifth were more than ten times greater, at 44 percent of total income. You would think that decades of targeted government programs, civil rights legislation, educational reform, and corrective national fiscal policy would result in tempering these differences. Forty years later, however, in 2017, the disparities were much more pronounced. The proportion of total income held by the lowest economic fifth had fallen by one-quarter of its 1977 total to 3.1 percent, while the highest fifth of American earners now took in 51.5 percent, almost seventeen times more, of all U.S. earnings. For an individual household, the trajectory has looked like this: a typical household in the lowest 20 percent bracket saw its (equivalence-adjusted) income rise by less than 8 percent in the forty years between 1977 and 2017 to $13,258, while a household in the highest 5 percent saw an income jump of 92 percent to $385,289. What's more, since 2000, the poorest 20 percent of the population has actually seen their income drop.

Race and gender continue to intersect with the picture of poverty. In household income, blacks currently make only 59 percent of what non-Hispanic whites earn; women of any race make 80.5 percent as much as men. It is not surprising, then, that women are more likely to be living in poverty (13.6 percent) than men (11 percent) or that the black poverty rate (21.2 percent) is more than double the rate for non-Hispanic whites.

When all this is taken together, one can only conclude that the national goal of achieving more economic equality is a compromised one. Our economic policies have resulted in much greater gains for those with more than for those with less, while those in the bottom tier of the economic system have recently been losing ground not just relatively but absolutely. As a result, poor people are less well positioned than ever before in recent history to be able to afford basic needs, especially housing.

Since 2000, not only has the median monthly income of low-income renters fallen by just over $100, but also the median monthly rent of low-income renters has increased by $60. "These renters," writes Brookings Institute researcher Jenny Schuetz, "are therefore getting squeezed by both declining incomes and rising rents, and finding that there is less money remaining for other expenses as a result."

What has happened to our country's poorest is that a growing percentage (figured in 2017 at 43 percent) are "severely rent burdened," the term HUD uses to refer to a household paying

50 percent or more of its income in rent. Among families in the bottom 20 percent by income, the median renter pays 56 percent of total income in rent, leaving only an estimated $476 per month after rent. This often makes it difficult to afford food, clothing, transportation, and medical care. It can drive renters into substandard housing that eats less of their income but is too inadequate or dangerous to be livable.

What's more, it leaves many in the vulnerable place where there is no way to save money and no way to weather even a small storm. Any misfortune—an unexpected medical bill, a layoff from your job or a cut in hours—can leave you short or late with your rent, often leading to eviction, as Matthew Desmond chronicled in *Evicted*, his Pulitzer Prize–winning book on this subject.

Burgeoning rents are a result of a housing shortfall attributed to multiple market factors, including an influx of millennials into the rental market as well as a flood of new renters who lost their homes after the 2008 mortgage crisis and subsequent recession. "Severe" housing problems have increased by 41 percent since the beginning of the recession. As the economy has recovered, new rental units have begun to bring relief to the market, but they primarily address the needs of high-income renters. The neediest are finding the supply of rental units deteriorating, in both numbers and quality. Should you be evicted, there are fewer and fewer units to be had once you are back on your feet, and a waiting list of eager renters for their landlords.

All of this is why so many Americans live on the edge of homelessness. And it is also why many you have met in this book have slid off the edge. The statistics in this chapter have flesh. They underlie the reason why Penelope was desperate enough for housing to pay rent for a room without any bathroom at all; why living in her storage unit (see chapter 5) seemed no worse. They explain why Miriam, whose grandfather was a local pioneer (see chapter 3), chose *"not so nice"* shelter life over an apartment in a neighborhood where, after she paid rent, she couldn't afford to use the heat or air-conditioning and was afraid of her neighbors. They are the numbers behind Kevin (see chapter 3), whose affordable rent ended when his landlord died and he found that his $772 Social Security income priced him out of the rental market. Living in the woods, he panhandles for supplemental income in the same parking lot where Randy (you met him in chapters 5 and 6) lives in his car recovering, we hope, from cancer. The statistics help to frame Ross's contention that his partially subsidized "welfare motel" rent was impoverishing him, and why he often felt more empowered and responsible living in the forest. You haven't met David, who worked his entire life without a pension and then lost his leg to diabetes, living for *nine years* in a cramped, filthy motel room where I first met him, before an affordable and accessible unit was finally found.

There were so many stories I didn't include of people living homeless who are still "on the list," waiting for vouchers or HUD housing for which they qualified but found there was either no voucher money left or no housing available. It is a startling fact that, as Schuetz writes, "unlike policies such as food stamps and Medicaid, housing assistance is not an entitlement for low-income families . . . Fewer than one in four eligible families receive federal help."

Up close, you see the web in which people are caught: how poverty contributes to homelessness but also how "deeply implicated," as Desmond has argued, is the lack of affordable housing in creating poverty. You can feel the frustration of homeless people who work full-time but cannot afford basic rent, and the irony of how shelters have become a way of subsidizing their low wages and even whole industries, like temp agencies, that depend on minimum wage workers. You see that all the factors that appear to contribute to homelessness—drug abuse, crime and incarceration, mental illness, unemployment—in fact cut both ways and are both effects and causes.

In the end, it is hard not to have a change of gaze. As a society, we create the conditions for a slippery slope causing countless individuals to slide into homelessness, yet we disavow the results. This is the greatest delusion, really, that some win, some lose, but the laws, institutions, and policies we support (or fail to support) have little to do with it.

My own gaze has shifted its focus on the causes of homelessness from misfits with personal problems to the human fallout from our economic system, and the systemic choices we have made and continue to make. This vantage point, more embedded in the web of conditions, makes it easier to see the continuity between the poor and the homeless and how their plight in our country is made more dire not just by my own lack of interest and understanding but by the profits being made off those who are the most down-and-out.

The High Cost of Being Poor

When Ross first mentioned "the high cost of being poor," I wasn't really sure what he meant. The worry of finances? The strain on relationships? The greater crime statistics in the neighborhood? What I came to see was that he wasn't referring to the personal toll that poverty and homelessness take but rather the counterintuitive reality that being poor costs money. In fact, there are a whole set of industries that make their profits from the money that only poor people pay.

It was just this week that Ross asked me to get a cashier's check for him so he could pay his rent. He had the money in hand, but the rental office doesn't take cash. It used to take money orders, which could be bought outside a bank, but there was an unexplained change in corporate policy. The real estate consortium that owns his complex will accept a personal check, but he doesn't have a bank account. It takes a cashier's check, which you can get from a bank, but only if you have a banking relationship.

Ross, like many other low-income Americans, is a member of "the unbanked," the term used by the financial industry to described that segment of the population who do not use the services of a bank, in which no one in the household, if there is a household, has a checking or savings account. It amounts to about 6.5 percent of all U.S. households.

Who are the unbanked? Not surprisingly, people who are "unbanked" are usually those who cannot afford to use bank services. The most commonly cited reason, in the FDIC's *National Survey of Unbanked and Underbanked Households,* was "Do not have enough money to keep in an account." They are people who cannot keep the minimum balance required to allow free checking; they often need their paycheck immediately and can't wait until it clears; they pay bills expecting income that either doesn't come or doesn't come on time, resulting in hefty overdraft fees they cannot afford. They are those in the United States whose incomes are both low and volatile, to the point where the irregularity of income becomes an issue. There is no money for an emergency.

This same national report shows how the unbanked manage their finances. Forty-five percent of those who are working will cash their paycheck in a place other than a bank; the working "unbanked are the primary users of the check-cashing industry." Unbanked households use cash (62.3 percent), non-bank money orders (35.5 percent), and prepaid debit cards (18.2 percent) to pay bills. They are the biggest users of prepaid cards because many do not have credit cards. In fact, 75.7 percent of unbanked individuals have "no credit" at all, and 16.4 percent use forms of "nonbank credit," such as pawn loans. The National Pawnbrokers Association estimates that approximately 40 percent of unbanked and underbanked households have used pawnshops for a loan (compared with 7.4 percent of all U.S. households in general).

The poor, in sum, certainly including the homeless, are the people whose financial lives depend on what the industry calls "alternative financial services": check cashing, payday loans, tax refund anticipation loans, rent-to-own services, pawnshop loans, and auto title loans. And these industries offer some of the most expensive financial products and services one can find.

I saw most of it up close through Ross's life. Not every alternative financial service was unreasonable. Come in with cash or a cash debit card, as Ross did, and you can get a money order to pay your bills. It cost him an envelope, a stamp, and sixty-nine cents. Cashing a payroll check usually involved additional fees. In his working years in town, Ross went to a gas station with a check cashing service, where he was charged 3 percent of his check to cash it. He considered that a good deal, and today there are even lower flat fees for the service as Walmart, among others, has gotten into the game. When Ross was in need of cash and didn't qualify for credit, he would pawn what valuables he had for a loan. But as you saw in the last chapter, he couldn't pay off the loan in full when it first came due—as is the case with most pawn borrowers. Then the real cost of pawn loans came into play. A full 80 percent of transactions nationwide come from these collateral loans in the pawn industry. To pay the finance charges on time, Ross often engaged in what he called "creative financing," selling some of his items of value—often for much less than they were worth—to keep his items in pawn so he wouldn't lose them.

When Ross and Wendi needed a larger amount, and they still had their car, they would go to an auto title loan outlet. In my town of fewer than 100,000 residents, there are nine auto title loan shops. *"These guys aren't cheap,"* Ross says. *"Most of the time the loan was the rent for the motel. It's like two hundred percent interest, and they keep the title until you pay up."*

Actually, the interest charged is much greater than Ross remembered. According to the website of the Federal Trade Commission:

> TITLE LOANS ARE EXPENSIVE. Lenders often charge an average of 25 percent per month to finance the loan. That translates to an APR of at least 300 percent. It could be higher, depending on additional fees that the lenders may require. For example, if you borrow $500 for 30 days, you could have to pay, on average, $125 plus the original $500 loan amount—$625 plus additional fees—within 30 days of taking out the loan.

The other thing learned from national data is how the loans tend to work out for consumers. One-fifth of all title loan borrowers lose their car. Eighty-three percent of loans are re-borrowed on the same day a previous loan is paid off. These re-borrowers are enmeshed in the same cycle of debt that you see in pawn loans, with debt going on for months. With title loans, half of borrowers re-borrow ten times or more; only one in eight pays the loan off in one cycle.

Many consider payday loans even worse. Two-thirds of payday loans are taken out by the working poor, including the homeless. According to the Consumer Federation of America, a typical loan (from $100 to $1,000, depending on state law) is for only two weeks, the length of a typical pay period. Their website explains:

"Loans typically cost 400% annual interest (APR) or more. The finance charge ranges from $15 to $30 to borrow $100. For two-week loans, these finance charges result in interest rates from 390 to 780% APR. Shorter term loans have even higher APRs. Rates are higher in states that do not cap the maximum cost."

In theory, when you get your paycheck, you will then pay off the "advance" plus interest. In reality, as the Pew Research Center shows, the average borrower will need 36 percent of his or her next paycheck to pay off the loan, when the borrower can afford just 5 percent, after paying for basic expenses. The result is that the loan can't usually be paid off, so there is an ongoing debt, with interest charges piling up.

There are more payday loan lenders now in the United States than McDonald's or Starbucks stores. Their loans account for more than two-thirds of the total revenues of the "alternative" lending industry. The shop where Ross and Wendi pawned their ring is owned by a company with thirty-five storefronts just in the state of Arizona. This company is only one of dozens of different pawnshops and chains that operate in this state alone; nationwide, there are more than ten thousand pawnshops. Auto title loan stores operate in twenty-five states with more than eight thousand loan stores. In 2018, fifty-five different companies offered online loans. "Check back," urges the loan lenders' website; "we're always adding new ones."

The Alternative Financial Service Providers Association, (whose website uses a dollar sign rather than an S for "Services" in its acronym—AF$PA) claims to represent the payday loan industry, boasting 64,000 U.S. locations, including a growing presence online. So does the Consumer Finance Service Association (CFSA), calling itself "the voice for payday loans," and FiSCA (Financial Service Centers of America), self-billed as the "industry's leading voice in the corridors of government in Washington, DC and throughout the country."

In fact, all of the alternative financial services industries maintain professional organizations whose main functions include representing the interests of their membership and industry through targeted programs of media and government relations. Many, like the National Pawnbrokers Association, also maintain PACs. You can get an idea from the website of a marketing analysis firm where those industry interests lie. It begins the publicly available portion of its industry report on "Check Cashing and Payday Loan (U.S.)" with three threats identified for the industry. In 2017 the first two threats were:

> Growth experienced during the recession will be hindered by increasing regulations.
> The most dangerous regulatory trend for operators is limiting interest rates on products.

Understanding how borrowers can become ensnared, Congress passed the Military Lending Act in 2015, which limited interest plus charges to 36 percent annually for military personnel and their spouses and dependents. In 2017 the Consumer Financial Protection Bureau finally took steps to further regulate the payday loan industry for the general public with the intention of stopping debt traps. Regulations would require lenders to determine if prospective borrowers can repay their debts, and the number of loans a lender may make to a borrower would be capped.

By the time you are reading this, you may or may not know whether these particular changes were successful. Since 2017, the payday loan industry has lobbied legislators to stop the law from becoming effective, arguing, as FiSCA asserts on its website, "[We] believe that Americans have a right to financial freedom that needs to be protected." In 2019, the very federal watchdog body responsible for proposing and enforcing the regulations, the Consumer Federal Protection Bureau (CFPB), under the Trump administration, "crippled the new rule," or as its website announced: "The CFPB has delayed the compliance date for the mandatory underwriting provisions in this rule to November 19, 2020, and has proposed to rescind those provisions."

In the coming years, these regulations—one way or the other—will become part of history, and there will be other issues and battles in this financial sector. I believe that most homeless people I have met would *not* like to see these industries shut down because these are often their only access to credit and financial services. What they want to be protected from is loans and services so usurious that they keep people in poverty or homelessness rather than help lift them from it. Ask for the suggestions of these end users in the industry—the people who actually take out loans, pawn their goods, rent to own, etc., and can see both industry benefits and drawbacks—and you will achieve a more balanced solution.

The alternative financial services industry, whose primary market is the poor, is a multibillion-dollar industry that will continue to be interested in the issues that affect its assets. It is crucial to our nation's health and humanity that we, the public, become interested too so that the path to the industry's survival will be much more of a middle road between profit and service.

In the End

All this leads me to the question of who we consider ourselves to be, and also who we do not. It strikes me that in our increasingly income-divided (and also politically divided) world, we have come to share fewer lived experiences and understandings. As pundits point out, this is in part because the marketers of products and services and information have so pinpointed our identities that we see only the realities that confirm our preferences and beliefs. In part, it is because most of our communities are no longer segregated by those who live on top of the (literal) hill versus those at the bottom, where we see each other in school or at the grocery store. Now those in various economic tiers have different zip codes, and schools, and grocery stores. There is an increasing sense of boundedness about who is us and who is them and a decreasing level of interaction between the camps.

These realities are relevant to the trajectory of homelessness, and specifically to the future of affordable housing. You can see what I mean when you realize that one of most significant obstacles to affordable housing is community opposition. On the HUD Exchange website (where HUD communicates with state and local governments, nonprofits, public housing authorities, tribes, and others), under the tab "Homeless Prevention and Assistance," is this overview: "Developing any kind of housing is a complicated process. There are issues such as site control, zoning, financing, environmental impacts, construction management, and operating costs to consider. When developing housing for homeless individuals, these issues are often secondary to a major impediment: community opposition, or NIMBYism."

"Not in my backyard" (NIMBY) opposition to affordable housing, according to the federal site, ranges from pressing for zoning restrictions to lobbying local officials, and from "exerting pressure on funding sources to withdraw financial support" to "vandalizing building sites in hopes of scaring off developers." One doesn't need to support these actions to understand them. Most people who oppose affordable housing are afraid. They fear that the safety and value of their neighborhoods will be sacrificed by allowing in people whose lives and circumstances they do not understand and do not identify with.

To overcome this, as well as to put in place the many other variables needed for affordable housing, will take more than a good fight, because in the end, even winning battles—when seen over time—are pyrrhic. The challenge will be to enlist rather than defeat opponents by a planning process that includes their concerns. I leave it to the readers of this book—who may be social workers and urban planners, church and temple members, or just good citizens—to find the solutions that fit your neighborhood. But I imagine that this process will, at the least, involve a social and physical architecture that does not ghettoize the poor or homeless, exacerbating our differences, or hide them from view. Organizations such as the National Alliance to End Homelessness offer valuable insights into working community solutions, and I rely on such information to keep apprised of the best practices in the changing political, legal, and social landscape of homelessness issues. Surely there are housing visions that can integrate our collective interests, and thoughtful policies that can provide the direction and incentives for us to rethink our community.

We can take a lesson in national public policy from Bhutan, whose focus is on Gross National Happiness (GNH) rather than Gross National Product (GNP) as the measure of progress. The system bases its GNH index on nine domains or "pillars," defined by thirty-three indicators which are regularly surveyed, including measures of living standards, health, and education, as well as more communal indices such as good governance, cultural diversity, and community vitality. For planning purposes, the index data can be broken down by any demographic characteristic or population group—men and women, rich and poor, city and rural—to determine where the shortfalls are the greatest as well as where the social contract is working. The stated goal for the nation is that all government projects and policies work together to maximize Gross National Happiness. National planning and resources follow the "suffering," addressing areas of greatest social need or inequity with the ultimate aim of fostering mutual human flourishing.

When I think of this more locally, the example that comes to mind in my town is a program designed to relieve suffering of homeless panhandlers while addressing questions of the common good. It takes on, in its design, the difficult question that I am commonly asked when people know I am in close contact with the homeless: Should I give money to a panhandler?

Most people want to help. But they are concerned that they are feeding someone's habit with their dollar or, worse for many, being scammed by someone too lazy to work. As a response to these concerns, a local group devised an innovative solution. To help people resolve the dilemma of giving and offer "a compassionate solution to panhandling," the group developed a program of "Better Bucks" to give to panhandlers. Here's how it works: You pay $6 for a "Better Buck" certificate book worth $5 and give out the certificates to panhandlers, who can redeem them at local businesses for food, clothing, transportation, and other basic items, not including alcohol or tobacco. Call it an attempt at Gross Local Happiness.

It sounds great, except when you talk to homeless people. It turns out that only a handful of businesses actually participate. This one gas station, that one grocery store, this deli, that shop, scattered all across the city. That's it, despite the fact that the program has been in existence for a few years. Why? Ross, along with other homeless people I surveyed, seems sure. The reason is that businesses don't want homeless people frequenting their locations. It is NIMBYism again, and the reason the program doesn't work.

So without a community commitment, we are left solely to our individual judgment. Here is how I think of it. There may in fact be some panhandlers who are "scamming," using some story or ruse to get quick money for alcohol or drugs or to avoid working. Then there are others, like most of the homeless people I have come to meet, for whom the money means their gas, food, medicine, car registration, the ability to get out of the cold for a couple of hours because they can buy a cup of coffee.

This means that for any encounter with a panhandler, there are two kinds of errors you can make as a benefactor. In one instance, you have given money to a scammer, or enabled someone's drinking habit. In the other, you have not given help to someone who could really use your dollar. Which error are you more willing to make? This is the question I ask myself all the time.

Perhaps all movement in social policy will begin with an inquiry and a commitment at the personal level first. One consequence of my slow but steady ten-year journey into the world of homeless people has been to put issues on my radar that had not previously been as central or visible in my life. Here are some of them: funding Section 8 housing vouchers; controlling usury; increasing the minimum wage; providing affordable housing incentives or mandates; ending racial inequity in sentencing and policing; decriminalizing camping and panhandling; enabling alcohol and drug abuse recovery programs; establishing day (as well as night) shelters; offering accessible low-cost health and mental health care; creating prison-to-work programs and other step-up programs from the shelters or jails or rehab centers into a useful education or a decent job.

There's a little quote written in my notes, part of an old interview with Ross about the "future" at a time when he was working as a house painter, living in the forest, trying to get medical help, saving for an apartment. "*The motivation of climbing back up,*" he said, "*it gets old.*" I remember writing that phrase verbatim because of the tiredness in his eyes as he said it, envisioning what it would take to extract himself one more time from his current life. I have seen that look in the eyes of other people who have been a part of this book. It was in Cal's eyes when he was speaking of his homeless past: "*It's not the first time I've been homeless, but each time you go through this, it just seems like the whole world—you lose everything.*" It comes from the shared experience of being homeless in this country and the common encounters one has, as Ross did, and as Jason and I witnessed.

Some of those encounters are captured in this book, others just in our memories. A full-time worker who must live in a shelter because she does not make enough money to afford housing in the town where she works. A recovering addict—just twenty-two years old—"graduated" from rehab with nowhere to go and no avenue toward a job or an education. A homeless temp worker who fears that reporting an injury will lose him a precious work "ticket." A onetime homeowner whose medical bills have left him living on the street. A government benefit that exists one year and is gone the next, as one administration comes and another goes. A young man hoping to pull himself out of the forest who can get help only if he represents himself as mentally ill. An older able-bodied man who must risk losing his food stamps to take an entry-level job that he is afraid may not last. A homeless couple who tell me they are followed every time they walk into the local drugstore. I remember Randy's words: that when he is panhandling, sometimes people shout things at him; but sometimes they don't look at him at all.

One day when I was walking in my neighborhood, a strapping young man, twenty-seven years old and Native American, looked in my direction, and I returned his gaze. He waited for that response before he walked over to me to ask for directions. He was lost, he told me, trying to get back to a housing complex I recognized as Section 8, where he had a friend. I decided to walk with him halfway to show him the route. As we walked, I learned his name was James. James told me he had been homeless since recently coming to town to find work, and this friend, an acquaintance really, let him sleep on the floor some nights. He panhandled for food money.

A few blocks into our walk, James said the most startling thing to me: *"I feel safe walking with you."* Why would a strong-looking guy like you feel safe with me? I thought and finally asked him out loud, not perceiving how my five-foot-two-inch frame could possibly help. The answer he gave was this:

> *I mean when it's just me, people look at me funny and they kind of follow me to see what I'm doing, and I don't feel I can really look at the houses and the cars. This is so nice because I can look at cars and houses and gardens and things that interest me when I'm with you.*

I have thought many times since of what underlay James's experience, and the best answer I have is "blindness and delusion." Ours.

None of us authoring this book is naïve enough to believe that discernment is unnecessary in our encounters with homeless. Sometimes caution and critical judgment are needed. But after the hundreds of homeless individuals we have met, and probably thousands of encounters we have witnessed or been told about, it is hard *not* to see our collective blindness and delusion, especially when it goes unexamined, as a form of violence.

One day while I was visiting Randy, he asked me if I wanted to meet another homeless car dweller in his parking lot. She received no government assistance, and lived in her car, panhandling during the day. They had befriended each other because she too had cancer. She was perhaps in her early forties. Randy introduced us, saying my name and then hers, as she sat with her rear door open, feet on the macadam of the parking lot. It was an acquaintance introducing an acquaintance to another acquaintance, but she knew I wasn't homeless like she or Randy was.

"I can't believe I'm in this position," was the first thing she said to me. *"I can't believe I'm living like this, out of my car. I'm so embarrassed."*

My heart quivered. I didn't know what to say. *"Why would you be embarrassed?"* finally came out of my mouth, and then I stuttered, *"There but for the grace of God . . ."* and she reached up and touched my shoulder before I finished: *"I wish everyone thought of it that way."* My words were a lie, really, because my economic and social capital would not likely ever leave me homeless. But the deeper truth in my message, *our* common humanity, came through anyway.

Perhaps that is really all that is needed. Think that people are like you. Think that you are like them. And see what comes from that. For me, it was this book.

Notes

1. The Beginning

5   More about our research methods. Both Jason and I went through standard IRB (Institutional Review Board)–approved research protocols to conduct our interviews. We approached, and invited the participation of, homeless individuals whom we saw staying in the town on more than a transient basis. Individuals were sometimes referred to us by another homeless person. There was no attempt to randomly sample the homeless population. Our interviews were all conducted in English, and we made an effort not to interview a person noticeably "under the influence" at the time of our conversation.

Formal interviews were recorded, when permitted by the participant, and the interviewees were usually compensated through some form of reciprocity, including cash, meals, restaurant vouchers, and bus passes. In all we conducted more than seventy-five formal interviews with forty-five individuals. Jason interviewed or surveyed twenty-four individuals who were attempting to get work at day labor companies, and Cathy conducted fifty-three interviews (twenty-four with Ross over a period of six years and twenty-nine other interviews between 2013–2018 with a total of twenty other homeless individuals). The names given to all people in this book aside from the authors are pseudonyms.

This book is also informed by a wider set of experiences with people who are homeless; Jason through his work as a day laborer and at a homeless shelter, Cathy through volunteer positions at different shelter facilities and many informal conversations with street dwellers and panhandlers, and Ross through his past and present life encounters.

2. The Road to Homelessness

8   *individual deviancy hypothesis* Vincent Lyon-Callo, *Inequality, Poverty, and Neoliberal Governance: Activist Ethnography in the Homeless Sheltering Industry* (Peterborough, Ont.: Broadview Press, 2004), 12. See also the connection between individual explanations of homelessness and capitalism in John R. Belcher and Bruce R. DeForge, "Social Stigma and Homelessness: The Limits of Social Change," *Journal of Human Behavior in the Social Environment* 22, no. 8 (2012): 929–46, https://doi.org/10.1080/10911359.2012.707941.

8   *self-help books* Jim Milliot, "The Hottest (and Coldest) Book Categories of 2014," *Publishers Weekly*, January 23, 2015, https://www.publishersweekly.com/pw/by-topic/industry news/bookselling/article/65387-the-hot-and-cold-categories-of-2014.html.
     Self-help books have remained strong sellers to the present, focusing recently on topics of "resilience." Catherine LaSota, "All the Feels: Self-Help Books, 2017–2018," *Publishers Weekly*, October 13, 2017, https://www.publishersweekly.com/pw/by-topic/new-titles/adult-announcements/article/75073-all-the-feels-self-help-books-2017-2018.html.

9   *"There is a cloud"* Thich Nhat Hanh, *The Heart of Understanding: Commentaries on the Prajnaparamita Heart Sutra*, 20th anniversary edition, ed. Peter Levitt (Berkeley: Parallax Press, 2009), 3–4.

10   *composite portraits* The scenarios do not represent single individuals and life histories, but rather are composite portraits drawn from themes and events that appear repeatedly in our interviews and in the literature. I present them this way because no set of actual individual stories in our interviews captured all the central themes that one repeatedly finds. Even these four composite portraits leave out certain recurring themes and trajectories. Composite portraits offered a vehicle to deliver patterns seen both in interview data and in national statistics. This is the only place in this book where composite information is used rather than actual individual history or encounters.

10   *"persistently poor"* Caroline Ratcliffe argues that the future achievement of ever-poor children is related to the length of time they live in poverty. Persistently poor children are 13 percent less likely to complete high school and 43 percent less likely to complete college than those who are poor but not persistently poor as children. Caroline Ratcliffe, *Child Poverty and Adult Success* (Washington, D.C.: Urban Institute, 2015), 3–4, https://www.urban.org/sites/default/files/publication/65766/2000369-Child-Poverty-and-Adult-Success.pdf.

10   *she was laid off as well* During this two-year period (2007–2009) alone, one in six workers was laid off, with layoffs disproportionately centered

on lower-education jobs. H. S. Farber, *Job Loss in the Great Recession: Historical Perspective from the Displaced Workers Survey, 1984–2010,* NBER Working Paper no. 17040 (Cambridge: National Bureau of Economic Research, 2011), http://www.nber.org/papers/w17040. It is also clear that job loss translates into homelessness. For instance, during the last recession, the number of families entering New York City homeless shelters jumped by 40 percent, in Minneapolis by 20 percent, in Los Angeles by 12 percent. The number of homeless families residing in state-supported shelters in Massachusetts rose 32 percent in one year, while shelters in Connecticut turned away 30 percent more families because of a lack of bed space. Barbara Sard, *Number of Homeless Families Climbing Due to Recession: Recovery Package Should Include New Housing Vouchers and Other Measures to Prevent Homelessness* (Washington, D.C.: Center on Budget and Policy Priorities, 2009), 2, https://www.cbpp.org/sites/default/files/atoms/files/1-8-09hous.pdf.

10 *headline in January 2009* Les Christie, "Foreclosures Up a Record 81% in 2008," CNNMoney.com, January 15, 2009, http://money.cnn.com/2009/01/15/real_estate/millions_in_foreclosure.

11 *61 percent rise in homelessness Homelessness in America: Overview of Data and Causes* (Washington, D.C.: National Law Center on Homelessness & Poverty, 2015), 3, https://nlchp.org//wp-content/uploads/2018/10/Homeless_Stats_Fact_Sheet.pdf.

11 *eviction due to foreclosure Renters in Foreclosure: A Fresh Look at an Ongoing Problem* (Washington, D.C.: National Low Income Housing Coalition, 2012), 1, https://nlihc.org/sites/default/files/Renters_in_Foreclosure_2012.pdf.

11 *crimes of possession* The number of arrests for possession *only* went from 538,100 in 1982 to 1,559,100 in 2006. "Drug and Crime Facts: Drug Law Violations—Enforcement," U.S. Department of Justice, n.d., https://www.bjs.gov/content/dcf/tables/salespos.cfm.

11 *82.5 percent of drug-related arrests* "Crime in the United States, 2006: Persons Arrested," U.S. Department of Justice, 2007, https://www2.fbi.gov/ucr/cius2006/arrests/index.html.

11 *African Americans accounted for 35 percent* "Crime in the United States, 2006," table 43, Arrests by Race.

11 *similar reported drug use* Blacks are three to four times more likely than whites to be arrested for drug crimes, even though they are no more likely to use or sell drugs. Jonathan Rothwell, "How the War on Drugs Damages Black Social Mobility," Brookings Institute, September 30, 2014, https://www.brookings.edu/blog/social-mobility-memos/2014/09/30/how-the-war-on-drugs-damages-black-social-mobility/.

11   *drug defendants adjudicated* "Drug and Crime Facts: Drug Law Violations—Pretrial, Prosecution, and Adjudication," U.S. Department of Justice, https://www.bjs.gov/content/dcf/ptrpa.cfm (accessed April 14, 2019).

11   *"ever" felon population* Sarah K. S. Shannon et al., "The Growth, Scope, and Spatial Distribution of People with Felony Records in the United States, 1948–2010," *Demography* 54, no. 5 (2017): 1795–1818, https://doi.org/10.1007/s13524-017-0611-1.

These same authors described the racially disproportionate growth of the ex-felon population over three decades: "The total number of non-African American ex-felons has grown from 2.5% of the adult population in 1980 to over 6% in 2010. For African-Americans, ex-felons have increased from 7.6% in 1980 to over 25% in 2010." Sarah Shannon et al., "Growth in the U.S. Ex-Felon and Ex-Prisoner Population, 1948–2010," paper presented at the Population Association of America annual meeting, Washington, D.C., April 1, 2011, http://paa2011.princeton.edu/papers/111687.

11   *In state court* Felony Sentences in State Courts, 2006—Statistical Tables (Washington, D.C.: U.S. Department of Justice, 2009), table 1.2, https://www.bjs.gov/content/pub/pdf/fssc06st.pdf.

12   *supportive family helped* Saneta deVuono-Powell et al., *Who Pays? The True Cost of Incarceration on Families* (Oakland: Ella Baker Center, Forward Together, Research Action Design, 2015), 9, http://www.ellabakercenter.org/sites/default/files/downloads/who-pays.pdf.

12   *employer conduct* According to a report from the Ella Baker Center, "formerly incarcerated individuals are far more likely to experience employer abuse in the workplace. Nearly half of respondents in this study reported experiencing some form of employer mistreatment, including wrongful termination (25%), wage theft (16%), wage discrimination (14%), and employer abuse (15%)." Saneta deVuono-Powell et al., *Who Pays?*, 21.

12   *finding work* Saneta deVuono-Powell et al., *Who Pays?*, 20.

12   *Men with criminal records* Binyamin Appelbaum, "Out of Trouble, but Criminal Records Keep Men Out of Work," *New York Times*, February 28, 2015, https://www.nytimes.com/2015/03/01/business/out-of-trouble-but-criminal-records-keep-men-out-of-work.html. Article statistics are based on *Non-Employed Poll* (Menlo Park: Kaiser Family Foundation, 2014), http://files.kff.org/attachment/kaiser-family-foundation-new-york-times-cbs-news-non-employed-poll-topline.

13   *unemployed or underemployed* Saneta deVuono-Powell et al., *Who Pays?*, 9.

13   *"most patriotic state"* Georgia had 0.92 enlistees per one thousand adults, the highest proportion in the nation, according to a compiled report tracking the average number of military enlistees (not officers) per one

thousand civilian adults between 2010 and 2015. Adam McCann, "2018's Most Patriotic States in America," WalletHub, June 26, 2018, https://wallethub.com/edu/most-patriotic-states/13680/#methodology.

The recruit-to-population ratio is higher in the South than in any other region of the country, according to the Heritage Foundation. Tim Kane, "Who Bears the Burden? Demographic Characteristics of U.S. Military Recruits Before and After 9/11," Heritage Foundation, November 7, 2005, https://www.heritage.org/defense/report/who-bears-the-burden-demographic-characteristics-us-military-recruits-and-after-911.

13   *disability payment* "Compensation: Veterans Compensation Benefits Rate Tables—Effective 12/1/11," U.S. Department of Veterans Affairs, last updated October 22, 2013, https://www.benefits.va.gov/COMPENSATION/resources_comp0111.asp.

The rate, figured from the vignette's time period of 2012, has risen to just $140 in 2019. "2019 VA Disability Rates," MilitaryBenefits.info, https://militarybenefits.info/va-disability-rates/ (accessed April 14, 2019).

A 10 percent disability award continues to be the most common for those who are determined to be disabled. Among the veterans designated as disabled through a rigorous application process, fewer than 10 percent will receive 100 percent of allowable disability payment benefits. Of the 284,550 veterans who successfully filed for benefits in 2016, 8.9 percent (25,427) of applicants received a disability rating of 100 percent. *Annual Benefits Report: Fiscal Year 2017* (Washington, D.C.: U.S. Department of Veterans Affairs, 2017), 74, https://www.benefits.va.gov/REPORTS/abr/docs/2017_abr.pdf.

13   *"doubling up" The State of Homelessness in America, 2016* (Washington, D.C.: National Alliance to End Homelessness, 2016), 3, http://endhomelessness.org/wp-content/uploads/2016/10/2016-soh.pdf.

For veterans who ended up in shelters, more than one in three had been living in such temporary arrangements with friends or family prior to becoming homeless. *Veteran Homelessness: A Supplemental Report to the 2010 Annual Homeless Assessment Report to Congress* (Washington, D.C.: U.S. Department of Housing and Urban Development and U.S. Department of Veterans Affairs, 2010), 22, https://www.va.gov/homeless/docs/2010aharveteransreport.pdf.

14   *"many from dual diagnosis"* "Veteran Homelessness Facts," Green Doors, http://www.greendoors.org/facts/veteran-homelessness (accessed April 14, 2019).

The percentages of veterans suffering from mental illness or substance abuse is much more than in either the general public or the non-veteran homeless population. Theresa Nguyen and Kelly Davis, *The*

State of Mental Health in America 2017 (Alexandria, Va.: Mental Health America, 2017), 5, https://www.mentalhealthamerica.net/sites/default/ files/2017%20MH%20in%20America%20Full.pdf. "Alcohol Facts and Statistics," National Institute of Alcohol Abuse and Alcoholism, last updated August 2018, https://www.niaaa.nih.gov/alcohol-health/ overview-alcohol-consumption/alcohol-facts-and-statistics.

For more on homelessness and veterans, see *The 2016 Annual Homeless Assessment Report (AHAR) to Congress*, pt. 1, *Point-in-Time Estimates of Homelessness* (Washington, D.C.: U.S. Department of Housing and Urban Development, 2016), https://www.hudexchange.info/resources/ documents/2016-AHAR-Part-1.pdf.

14   *As social networks retreat* Along with mental health issues and substance abuse, significant risk factors for homelessness among veterans are lack of support and social isolation after discharge. Jack Tsai and Robert Rosenheck cite three different rigorous studies in which lack of social support emerged as a risk factor for homelessness among veterans. Jack Tsai and Robert A. Rosenheck, "Risk Factors for Homelessness among US Veterans," *Epidemiologic Reviews* 37, no. 1 (2015): 181, https://doi. org/10.1093/epirev/mxu004.

14   *share two characteristics* In 2016, for instance, the poverty rate for civilian veterans with disabilities aged eighteen to sixty-four years living in the community was 17.6 percent, while the poverty rate for civilian veterans without disabilities aged eighteen to sixty-four living in the community was 6.5 percent—a significant poverty gap of 11.1 percentage points. "2017 Annual Disability Statistics Compendium," Institute on Disability/UCED, table 5.5, https://disabilitycompendium.org/ compendium/2017-annual-disability-statistics-compendium (accessed April 14, 2019).

14   *fewer opportunities growing up* On one level, one might expect that veterans born poor, just like those born poor in the general population, are more likely to be homeless because their opportunities and the economic safety nets that families can provide are more limited. In Robert's case, his lower socioeconomic upbringing in the rural South made it difficult for him to pursue higher education and constrained his post-military earning power; his PTSD further eroded his financial possibilities. But the intersection of poverty and homelessness also explains why "roughly 45% of all homeless veterans are African American or Hispanic, despite only accounting for 10.4% and 3.4% of the U.S. veteran population, respectively." "Background & Statistics: FAQ about Homeless Veterans," National Coalition for Homeless Veterans, http://nchv.org/index.php/ news/media/background_and_statistics/ (accessed April 14, 2019).

14   *military pay grade* In their population-based cohort study of 310,685 veterans who served in Iraq and Afghanistan, Stephen Metraux and his associates assessed baseline risk factors for homelessness among veterans, finding that PTSD was "a significant factor of modest magnitude for homelessness" but that "pay grade, as a proxy for socioeconomic status, was a strong and consistent risk factor for becoming homeless." They conclude that "the 44% of the study cohort who were in the lowest pay grade category (E1–E4) accounted for 72% of those becoming homeless." And "the risk of becoming homeless among those in the higher pay grade categories was 9% compared with 43% among those in the lowest pay grade category (E1–E4)." Stephen Metraux et al., "Risk Factors for Becoming Homeless among a Cohort of Veterans Who Served in the Era of the Iraq and Afghanistan Conflicts," *American Journal of Public Health* 103, no. S2 (2013): S255–61, https://doi.org/10.2105/AJPH.2013.301432.

14   *one in every six homeless people* The figures reported for Arizona veterans' homelessness during this time period are from *Veteran Homelessness: A Supplemental Report to the 2010 Annual Homeless Assessment Report to Congress* (Washington, D.C.: U.S. Department of Housing and Urban Development, U.S. Department of Veterans Affairs, 2010), https://www.va.gov/homeless/docs/2010aharveteransreport.pdf.

Although the great majority of veterans are not homeless, they are still more likely than the general population to be homeless. Jamison Fargo et al., "Prevalence and Risk of Homelessness among US Veterans," *Preventing Chronic Disease* 9 (2012): 110–12, http://dx.doi.org/10.5888/pcd9.110112.

14   *unsheltered on the streets* Carol Wilkins and Janice Elliott, *Supplemental Document to the Federal Strategic Plan to Prevent and End Homelessness: June 2010, Background Paper—Veterans Homelessness* (Washington, D.C.: U.S. Interagency Council on Homelessness, 2010), www.usich.gov/resources/uploads/asset_library/BkgrdPap_Veterans.pdf.

15   *domestic violence* "Domestic Violence and Homelessness," National Coalition for the Homeless, last modified February 21, 2012, http://www.national homeless.org/factsheets/domestic.html.

16   *"cost (or rent) burdened"* Leighton Walter Kille, "The State of the Nation's Housing, 2014: Rentals Up, Homeownership Down, Minorities Become a Force," *Journalist's Resource*, July 23, 2014, https://journalistsresource.org/studies/economics/real-estate/the-state-of-the-nations-housing-2014.

16   *"half their incomes in rent"* "Harvard's Joint Center for Housing Studies Report Shows Lack of Affordable Rental Housing," National Low Income Housing Coalition, June 26, 2017, http://nlihc.org/article/harvard-s-joint-center-housing-studies-report-shows-lack-affordable-rental-housing.

An updated report and interactive data tables can be found on Harvard's website. See "The State of the Nation's Housing 2018," Joint Center for Housing Studies of Harvard University, https://www.jchs.harvard.edu/state-nations-housing-2018 (accessed April 20, 2019).

16   *seventy hours a week* The hours of work needed to afford a modest rental was figured on the 2016 minimum wage. You can find a more recent interactive chart at "Out of Reach 2018," National Low Income Housing Coalition, http://nlihc.org/oor (accessed October 2, 2017).

To read the full written report detailing state-by-state housing findings, see Andrew Aurand et al., *Out of Reach 2017: The High Cost of Housing* (Washington, D.C.: National Low Income Housing Coalition, 2017), http://nlihc.org/sites/default/files/oor/OOR_2017.pdf.

16   *15 percent of all homeless adults* Hunger and Homelessness Survey: A Status Report on Hunger and Homelessness in America's Cities (Washington, D.C.: U.S. Conference of Mayors, 2014), https://www2.cortland.edu/dotAsset/655b9350-995e-4aae-acd3-298325093c34.pdf.

17   *Homophobia is a leading cause* Research suggests that "although LGB youths compose only 1.4%–5.0% of the general youth population[,] LGB youths compose 15%–36% of homeless youths." Margaret Rosario, Eric W. Schrimshaw, and Joyce Hunter, "Risk Factors for Homelessness among Lesbian, Gay, and Bisexual Youths: A Developmental Milestone Approach," *Children and Youth Services Review* 34, no. 1 (2012): 186–93, https://doi.org/10.1016/j.childyouth.2011.09.016.

A study in the Massachusetts public schools showed that LGBT teens were between four and thirteen times more likely to be homeless than their exclusively heterosexual peers. Heather L. Corliss et al., "High Burden of Homelessness among Sexual Orientation Minority Adolescents: Findings from a Representative Massachusetts Sample," *American Journal of Public Health* 101 (2011): 1683–89, https://doi.org/10.2105/AJPH.2013.301432.

17   *Medical problems and costs* Seiji Hayashi, "How Health and Homelessness Are Connected—Medically," *The Atlantic*, January 25, 2016, https://www.theatlantic.com/politics/archive/2016/01/how-health-and-homelessness-are-connectedmedically/458871/.

A 2013 NerdWallet health analysis report found that more than half of U.S. bankruptcies, a precipitating condition of some homelessness, are caused by medical issues. Dan Mangan, "Medical Bills Are the Biggest Cause of US Bankruptcies: Study," CNBC, July 24, 2013, https://www.cnbc.com/id/100840148.

17   *significant number of homeless* The Second Annual Homeless Assessment Report to Congress (Washington, D.C.: U.S. Department of

Housing and Urban Development, 2008), iv, https://www.hudexchange. info/resources/documents/2ndHomelessAssessmentReport.pdf.

17   *underpinnings* Daniel Weinberger, "The Causes of Homelessness in America," Stanford University, last modified July 26, 1999, https://web. stanford.edu/class/e297c/poverty_prejudice/soc_sec/hcauses.htm.

17   *"blames the victim"* Judith Treas, "The Great American Recession: Sociological Insights on Blame and Pain," *Sociological Perspectives* 53, no. 1 (2010): 3–17, https://doi.org/10.1525/sop.2010.53.1.3.

18   *one-in-two-hundred chance* This statistic, and the other projected odds of homelessness in this chapter, unless otherwise noted, are cited by Donna Kimura, "Study: More Americans Are Homeless, *Affordable Housing Finance,* January 1, 2011, retrieved from https://www.housingfinance. com/news/study-more-americans-are-homeless_o. The data come from the prior year's (2010) *State of Homelessness in America* report put out by the National Alliance to End Homelessness. More recent annual reports can be found at www.endhomelessness.org.

18   *odds of being born poor* Kayla Fontenot, Jessica Semega, and Melissa Kollar, *Income and Poverty in the United States* (Washington, D.C.: U.S. Census Bureau, 2018), 12, https://www.census.gov/content/dam/Census/ library/publications/2018/demo/p60-263.pdf.

18   *One in five people* Cliff Van Zorn, Cliff Zukin, and Allison Kopicki, *Left Behind: The Long-Term Unemployed Struggle in an Improving Economy* (New Brunswick: Rutgers University Edward J. Bloustein School of Planning and Public Policy, John J. Heldrich Center for Workforce Development, 2014), http://www.heldrich.rutgers.edu/products/left-behind-long-term-unemployed-struggle-improving-economy.

18   *chances of being laid off* The Pew Research Center reported this at the height of the recession, finding that "about two-in-ten adults with no more than a high school education say they lost a job last year [2007]—a job loss rate three times greater than the rate among college graduates and significantly greater than the loss rate of those who went to college but did not graduate." "You're Laid Off: A Worsening Economy Couldn't Come at a Worse Time for Many U.S. Workers," Pew Research Center, April 16, 2008, http://www.pewsocialtrends.org/2008/04/16/youre-laid-off/.

20   *Kim Hopper* To see an interview with Hopper on the topic of homelessness and poverty, check out Kim Hopper with Barbara Ehrenreich, "Homeless and Poor in America: Implications for Healthcare," YouTube, March 10, 2008, https://www.youtube.com/watch?v=aJibJh-1unk.

20   *Domestic abuse, drug or alcohol addiction* With regard to domestic violence by an intimate partner, one in seven women and one in twenty-five men have suffered abuse serious enough that they have been physically

injured. "Domestic Violence," National Coalition Against Domestic Violence, n.d., https://www.speakcdn.com/assets/2497/domestic_violence2.pdf.

According to the "Alcohol Facts and Statistics" from the National Institutes of Health, National Institute on Alcohol Abuse, in 2015, 27 percent of U.S. adults had engaged in binge drinking in the past month and 7 percent in heavy alcohol use, and 6.7 percent of the U.S. population eighteen and older was considered to have alcohol use disorder. "Alcohol Facts and Statistics," National Institute of Alcohol Abuse and Alcoholism, last updated August 2018, https://www.niaaa.nih.gov/alcohol-health/overview-alcohol-consumption/alcohol-facts-and-statistics.

Although drug abuse statistics are less reliable than those for alcohol abuse because people don't self-report, more people die now from drug use than from drinking. The Center for Disease Control estimates that in 2016, the percentage of Americans who used illegal drugs was 10.6 percent. "Table 50. Use of selected substances in the past month among persons aged 12 and over, by age, sex, race, and Hispanic origin: United States, selected years 2002–2016" (Washington, D.C.: Centers for Disease Control and Prevention, 2017), https://www.cdc.gov/nchs/data/hus/2017/050.pdf.

From 1999 to 2017, the rate of drug overdose deaths in the United States more than tripled (from 6.1 per 100,000 to 21.7), and the statistics show the recent acceleration of the addiction problem. On average, overdose deaths increased by 10 percent per year from 1999 through 2006, by 3 percent per year from 2006 through 2014, and by 16 percent per year from 2014 through 2017. Overdose deaths involving synthetic opioids increased 45 percent just from 2016 to 2017. Holly Hedegaard, Arialdi M. Miniño, and Margaret Warner, *Drug-Overdose Deaths in the United States, 1999–2017,* National Center for Health Statistics Data Brief (no 329) (Washington, D.C.: National Center for Health Statistics, November 2018) https://www.cdc.gov/nchs/data/databriefs/db329-h.pdf.

According to the "Mental Health in America 2017" report, one in five adults has a mental health condition. Nguyen and Davis, *The State of Mental Health in America 2017*, 5.

22   *connection between mental illness* To read more about the relationship between homelessness and mental illness, see Kim Hopper, "More Than a Passing Strange: Homelessness and Mental Illness in New York City," *American Ethnologist* 15, no. 1 (1988): 155–67, http://dx.doi.org/10.1525/ae.1988.15.1.02a00100. See also Kim Hopper, *Reckoning with Homelessness* (Ithaca: Cornell University Press, 2002).

23   *product of the larger system* Martha R. Burt, *Over the Edge: The Growth of Homelessness in the 1980s* (New York: Russell Sage Foundation, 1993).

3. The Stigma of Homelessness

24   *after they were edited for synonyms* Different words with close to the same meaning, such as Poor and Broke, were combined and counted as the same concept. Similarly, different spellings or versions of a word, such as Ragged and Raggedy, were combined as one.

26   *American cultural narratives* Teresa Gowan, *Hobos, Hustlers, and Backsliders: Homeless in San Francisco* (Minneapolis: University of Minnesota Press, 2010).

27   *"master status"* Jason Adam Wasserman and Jeffrey Michael Clair, *At Home on the Street: People, Poverty, and a Hidden Culture of Homelessness* (Boulder: Lynne Rienner Publishers, 2010).

27   *"distancing"* David A. Snow and Leon Anderson, "Identity Work among the Homeless: The Verbal Construction and Avowal of Personal Identities," *American Journal of Sociology* 92, no. 6 (1987): 1336–71, https://www.jstor.org/stable/2779840. And see also their classic work David A. Snow and Leon Anderson, *Down on Their Luck: A Study of Homeless Street Dwellers*, (Berkeley: University of California Press, 1993).

29   *When I asked her* I do not generally offer any details of my conversations with shelter dwellers because my role with them was as a volunteer and support, not as a researcher. I did not take notes at the overflow shelter, nor did I interview people. In Miriam's case, I encountered her outside the shelter and received her permission to conduct one formal interview, the contents of which are used here and earlier in the chapter, and to include in the research my memory of our prior conversations.

31   *"houseless"* "Houseless, Not Homeless!," http://www.houseless.org/ (accessed July 29, 2017).

32   *laws that prevent or limit panhandling* While the Supreme Court struck down city restrictions on begging in August 2017, local policy and legislation had been traveling in the opposite direction. City restrictions on panhandling had increased markedly since 2006 (61 percent restricted panhandling in certain public spaces, according to a 2016 study of 187 cities), and many city officials claimed that the 2017 ruling, while it preserved free speech, would present serious health and safety risks. Joe Palazzolo, "As Panhandling Laws Are Overturned, Cities Change Policies," *Wall Street Journal*, August 8, 2017, https://www.wsj.com/articles/as-panhandling-laws-are-overturned-cities-change-policies-1502204399.

34   *"You can see me?"* The story can be found at "About Us," Invisible People, https://invisiblepeople.tv/about/ (accessed April 20, 2019).

35   *volunteered in a church shelter* I volunteered at the church shelter during two winter seasons before becoming a more regular weekly volunteer at the Community Shelter.

38   *"homeless people you'll ignore today"* "About Us," https://invisiblepeople.
      tv/about/.

4. A Sheltered, Homeless Day

49   *storage unit* This shelter allows you to leave items in storage for three
      days after you were last in residence. Kyle will negotiate with clients,
      though, for extenuating circumstances such as being pulled into jail, so
      clients will not lose their possessions. In most cases, though, items left in
      storage longer than the grace period are discarded.

56   *deaths of homeless have soared* Tim Craig, "Homeless Deaths Surge: Opioids,
      Extreme Weather, Soaring Housing Costs Contribute to the Spike across the
      Country," *Washington Post*, April 13, 2018, https://www.washingtonpost.
      com/news/national/wp/2018/04/13/feature/surge-in-homeless-deaths-
      linked-to-opioids-extreme-weather-soaring-housing-cost.

59   *alcohol and drugs* The shelter has applied for grants that would enable it
      to expand, allowing it to add additional beds, admit families, and desig-
      nate a special "sober" area of the shelter.

5. On the Street

60   *unsheltered homeless* For the HUD definition of unsheltered homeless,
      see "Definitions of Homelessness for Federal Program Serving
      Children, Youth, and Families," U.S. Department of Health and
      Human Services, n.d., https://www.acf.hhs.gov/sites/default/files/ecd/
      homelessness_definition.pdf.

61   *severely undercounted* The National Law Center on Homelessness and
      Poverty estimates that the actual numbers could be from two to ten
      times higher than the formal count. *Don't Count on It: How the HUD
      Point-in-Time Count Underestimates the Homelessness Crisis in America*
      (Washington, D.C.: National Law Center on Homelessness and Poverty,
      2017), https://www.nlchp.org/documents/HUD-PIT-report2017.

61   *increased again in 2018* The 2018 *Annual Homeless Assessment Report
      (AHAR) to Congress*, pt. 1, *Point-in-Time Estimates of Homeless-
      ness* (Washington, D.C.: U.S. Department of Housing and Urban
      Development, 2018), https://www.hudexchange.info/resources/
      documents/2018-AHAR-Part-1.pdf.

61   *one national report* The 2015 *Annual Homeless Assessment Report
      (AHAR) to Congress*, pt. 2, *Estimates of Homelessness in the United
      States* (Washington, D.C.: U.S. Department of Housing and Urban
      Development, 2015), https://www.hudexchange.info/onecpd/assets/
      File/2014-AHAR-Part-2.pdf.

64   *the advantage of tunnels* The classic work describing people living in tunnels is Jennifer Toth's book *The Mole People: Life in the Tunnels beneath New York City* (Chicago: Chicago Review Press, 1993). More recently, Matthew O'Brien shares his encounters, albeit in a sensationalized fashion, with unsheltered homeless people in *Beneath the Neon: Life and Death in the Tunnels of Las Vegas* (Las Vegas: Huntington Press, 2007).

67   *we both know this is illegal* This changed in September 2018, when the Ninth Circuit Court of Appeals sided with six homeless residents of Boise, Idaho, who argued they were unable to comply with city rulings against camping when shelters were full because they had no place else to go. The court said such ordinances amount to "cruel and unusual punishment" when homeless are made to choose between following the law or sleeping. *Martin v. City of Boise*, no. 15–35845 (9th Cir. 2018).

70   *outlaw shopping carts* Jim Schutze, "We've Banned Their Shopping Carts, Outlawed Panhandling, Provided Homes for the Homeless— And Nothing's Worked. There May Be One Modest Proposal That Solves the Problem," *Dallas Observer*, September 2, 2010, https://www. dallasobserver.com/news/weve-banned-their-shopping-carts-outlawed-panhandling-provided-homes-for-the-homeless-and-nothings-worked-there-may-be-one-modest-proposal-that-solves-the-problem-6419206.

77   *massive cuts* The estimates were according to a summer 2018 report from the Center on Budget and Policy Priorities (CBPP), a progressive U.S. organization that analyzes the impact of federal and state government budget policies. They were based on cuts that were part of the farm bill passed by the House of Representatives but still being negotiated by the Senate in summer 2018. "A Quick Guide to SNAP Eligibility and Benefits," Center on Budget and Policy Priorities, last modified October 16, 2018, https://www.cbpp.org/research/food-assistance/a-quick-guide-to-snap-eligibility-and-benefits.

The farm bill became law on December 20, 2018 and, although many expected restrictions on SNAP eligibility did not materialize, the SNAP Data Tables from the U.S. Department of Agriculture show that the average monthly benefit per person as of July 2019 was, as the CBPP predicted, $134.85. "SNAP Data Tables: FY15 through FY18 *National View Summary*," Food and Nutrition Service, U.S. Department of Agriculture, data as of July 5, 2019, https://www.fns.usda.gov/pd/ supplemental-nutrition-assistance-program-snap.

6. Making Money

83   *five to eight times* Robert C. James and Cameron A. Mustard, "Geographic Location of Commercial Plasma Donation Clinics in the United States,

1980–1995," *American Journal of Public Health* 94, no. 7 (2004): 1224–29, https://ajph.aphapublications.org/doi/10.2105/AJPH.94.7.1224.

83   *"number of centers in the United States"* Darryl Lorenzo Wellington reports total donations leaping from 12.5 million in 2006 to more than 23 million in 2011. Darryl Lorenzo Wellington, "The Twisted Business of Donating Plasma," *The Atlantic,* May 28, 2014, https://www.theatlantic.com/health/archive/2014/05/blood-money-the-twisted-business-of-donating-plasma/362012/.

83   *"least restrictive plasma regulations"* H. Luke Shaefer and Analidis Ochoa, "How Blood-Plasma Companies Target the Poorest Americans," *The Atlantic,* March 15, 2018, https://www.theatlantic.com/business/archive/2018/03/plasma-donations/555599/.

84   *more than six hundred donation centers* "Over a decade, the number of donations—really, 'sales' is a more accurate noun—in America tripled, from 12 million per year in 2006 to 38 million per year in 2016, according to the Plasma Protein Therapeutics Association, a trade group. The number of donation centers in the U.S. has more than doubled to meet demand, from fewer than 300 sites in 2005 to over 600 today [2018]. Global sales jumped from $5 billion in 2000 to $20 billion in 2015, and are expected to keep growing at a rapid clip well into the next decade." Shaefer and Ochoa, "How Blood-Plasma Companies Target the Poorest Americans."

84   *U.S. donors supply 70 percent* Shaefer and Ochoa, "How Blood-Plasma Companies Target the Poorest Americans." The authors' claim is based on a 2006 report (updated 2009) from the Australian Department of Health. Philip Flood, Peter Wills, Sir Peter Lawler, Graeme Ryan, and Kevin A. Rickard, *Review of Australia's Plasma Fractionation Arrangements* (Barton, Australia: Commonwealth of Australia, updated May 21, 2009), https://www1.health.gov.au/internet/main/publishing.nsf/Content/B3B4E1D741764DD2CA257BF000193A6F/$File/plasma_FINAL%20as%20at%2030%20November%202006.pdf.

84   *"One of the best ways"* "How to Make Money Donating Plasma When Homeless," HomelessAdvice.com, August 1, 2018, https://homelessadvice.com/how-to-make-money-donating-plasma-when-homeless/.

84   *laws criminalizing begging* Since a 2015 Supreme Court ruling related to signage and free speech, panhandling laws that limit the ability of people to ask for donations through speech or signs have become more contestable. Dozens of cities have repealed their begging laws to head off litigation, according to Joe Palazzolo, "As Panhandling Laws Are Overturned," *Wall Street Journal,* August 8, 2017.

88   *interviews and survey research* Jason's research includes interviews with seventeen day laborers (ten of whom also filled out detailed

questionnaires on their personal and work history and/or daily schedules) along with seven other laborers who just provided written information.

89   *hiring entry-level workers* The trend toward industries shifting to temporary labor for entry-level hires has been particularly apparent in the years of growth following the recession. Temporary employment levels increased as companies, cautious about their chances for a sustained recovery, incorporated temporary staffing models into permanent corporate policy. According to Susan H. Houseman and Carolyn J. Heinrich, from June 2009 to late 2015, the temp help industry alone accounted for over 13 percent of net employment gains; see their *Temporary Help Employment in Recession and Recovery* (Kalamazoo, Mich.: W. E. Upjohn Institute for Employment Research, 2015), 1, https://doi.org/10.17848/wp15-227. For more on this trend, see Laura Newberry, "Temp Jobs Become Way to Go for Many Employers," *USA Today*, August 16, 2013, https://www.usatoday.com/story/money/business/2013/08/16/economy-temporary-workers/2665645/. Also see Sarah Gardner, "The Temp Industry Is at an All-Time High," *Marketplace*, June 17, 2016, https://www.marketplace.org/2016/05/31/world/profits-temps.

The U.S. Bureau of Labor Statistics reported a record 3 million temp employees for the month of July 2018 alone. "Employment, Hours, and Earnings from the Current Employment Statistics Survey (National): Temporary Help Services," Bureau of Labor Statistics, https://data.bls.gov/timeseries/CES6056132001 (accessed April 20, 2019).

More recently, the American Staffing Association reported its companies hire more than 17 million temporary and contract employees every year. "Staffing Industry Statistics: Staffing Employees," American Staffing Association, https://americanstaffing.net/staffing-research-data/fact-sheets-analysis-staffing-industry-trends/staffing-industry-statistics/ (accessed April 20, 2019).

89   *less than for the average American* According to the 2015 U.S. Census, 33 percent of Americans had a bachelor's degree, 88 percent had a high school diploma, and 59 percent had some college. Camille L. Ryan and Kurt Bauman, *Educational Attainment in the United States: 2015* (Washington, D.C.: U.S. Census Bureau, 2016), 1, https://www.census.gov/library/publications/2016/demo/p20-578.html.

91   *staffing industry actively promotes* The American Staffing Association website highlights the positive connection between temp labor and a permanent job. Citing its own surveys, it highlights statistics such as the fact that half of all temp workers believe it is a path to a permanent job and nine out of ten say that temp work made them more employable. "Staffing Industry Statistics: Staffing Employees."

100 *injured at a higher rate* A ProPublica analysis of worker's compensation claims in five states found the incidence of workplace injuries was
between 36 percent and 73 percent higher for temporary workers than
for non-temporary workers. Olga Pierce, Jeff Larson, and Michael Gra-
bell, "How We Calculated Injury Rates for Temp and Non-Temp Workers," ProPublica, December 18, 2013, https://www.propublica.org/nerds/
how-we-calculated-injury-rates-for-temp-and-non-temp-workers.

102 *hardly enough to rent a room* The mean hourly wage of wage and salary
workers in our town in May 2017 was $20.53, which equates to a mean
salary of $42,702 (calculated at 2,080 hours a year), or $3,559 per month.
"Occupational Employment and Wages in [Redacted]—May 2017,"
Bureau of Labor Statistics, last modified April 26, 2018, https://www.bls.
gov/regions/west/home.htm.

7. Navigating the Bureaucracy

104 *"Please come in"* Ross provided his permission to the housing office for
me to attend and take notes in his session.

104 *six characteristics of a bureaucracy* Weber argues that the bureaucratic orga-
nizational form is characterized by these features: (1) specialization and
division of labor; (2) hierarchical authority structures; (3) rules and regulations; (4) technical competence guidelines; (5) impersonality and personal
indifference; (6) a standard of formal written communications. Max Weber,
Economy and Society: An Outline of Interpretive Sociology, ed. Guenther Roth
and Claus Wittich (Berkeley: University of California Press, 1978).

108 *"street-level bureaucrats"* Michael Lipsky, *Street-Level Bureaucracy: Dilemmas
of the Individual in Public Service* (New York: Russell Sage Foundation, 1980).

110 *your chances* On the probability of successfully obtaining Social Security
disability income, see Deborah Dennis et al., "Helping Adults Who Are
Homeless Gain Disability Benefits: The SSI/SSDI Outreach, Access, and
Recovery (SOAR) Program," *Psychiatric Services* 62, no. 11 (2011): 1373–
76, as cited in Matthew D. Marr, *Better Must Come: Exiting Homelessness
in Two Global Cities* (Ithaca: Cornell University Press, 2015), 80.

110 *those who are approved* The information about successful versus unsuccessful SSDI applicants comes from Marr's interview with a lead SSI case
manager in Los Angeles. Marr, *Better Must Come,* 81–82.

110 *"cooperative and deserving"* Marr, *Better Must Come,* 84.

8. Home at Last

119 *federal subsidies for their housing* Ross's rent is subsidized under the Section 8 housing choice voucher program. "The largest component of

today's Section 8 program, the voucher program, was first authorized by the Housing and Urban-Rural Recovery Act of 1983 (P.L. 98–181). It was originally a demonstration program, but was made permanent in 1988." *An Overview of the Section 8 Housing Programs: Housing Choice Vouchers and Project-Based Rental Assistance* (Washington, D.C.: Congressional Research Service, 2014), 5, https://www.everycrsreport. com/files/20140207_RL32284_c06c87f7a9b055ade32ee0ca1e2bd69c-17c89ecb.pdf. "The federal government currently funds more than 2 million Section 8 Housing Choice Vouchers [officially named in 1998]. PHAs [public housing agencies] administer the program and receive an annual budget from HUD. Each has a fixed number of vouchers that they are permitted to administer, and they are paid administrative fees . . . Vouchers are tenant-based in nature, meaning that the subsidy is tied to the family, rather than to a unit of housing . . . Families no longer qualify for a subsidy when their incomes, which must be recertified annually, have risen to the point that 30% of that income is equal to rent" (7–8).

120   *housing choice voucher program* "United States Fact Sheet: Federal Rental Assistance," *Center on Budget and Policy Priorities*, March 30, 2017, https://www.cbpp.org/sites/default/files/atoms/files/4-13-11hous-US. pdf.

123   *"The Cupboard"* Only a year after The Cupboard opened in 2018, it closed because of regulatory issues that could not be resolved by the parties involved. The problem boiled down to the fact that the organization did not have the right category of nonprofit status that would allow supermarkets and megastores, the main contributors of food, to write off their contributions. Another nonprofit organization took The Cupboard's operation under its umbrella temporarily, reopening it in 2019 in a new location until it will be able to spin off as a separate entity once again.

126   *selling items that people pawn* By its own admission, the pawn industry asserts that "pawnbrokers' core business is making collateral loans." Eighty percent of pawnbrokers report that collateral loans are the most common transactions made. "Pawnbrokers Report Decrease in Retail Sales as Online Competition Grows and Buying Trends Shift," National Pawnbrokers Association, May 30, 2017, https://www. nationalpawnbrokers.org/2017/pawnbrokers-report-decrease-in-retail-sales-as-online-competition-grows-and-buying-trends-shift/.

128   *interest is heavily front-loaded* By my calculation, 75 percent of the total interest due at the loan's end would be owed in zero to thirty days, should a pawn customer wish to pay off early.

128   *follow the math* Ross and Wendi have already renewed their loan several times this year at two-month intervals. So if they continue to pay

off their $64.33 in interest every two months, they will have done this five times in a year before their final payment, paying total interest of $321.65. The final two-month payment must include an interest payment plus a storage fee plus the amount of the initial loan, so they will hand over a lump payment of $291.50, bringing their total costs for the year for a $225 loan to $613.15 (reflecting a total interest amount of $388.15). This is a 172 percent annual interest rate.

129   *your company will quickly grow* Mike Katsanevas, "Dollars and Sense: Creating an Annual Budget," *National Pawnbroker* (Fall 2015), https://issuu.com/nationalpawnbrokers/docs/npa_mag_fall2015_hr__1_.

9. Blind and Delusional

132   *other worlds I have entered* My ethnographic work, captured in two editions (1997 and 2011) of *Voyages: From Tongan Villages to American Suburbs* (Ithaca: Cornell University Press), included living in a village in the kingdom of Tonga between 1981 and 1984, returning several times to look at changes in village life due to globalization. I also lived in a college dormitory for a year, in 2002–2003, while taking classes posing as a freshman, to understand the challenges of undergraduate life, resulting in the book *My Freshman Year: What a Professor Learned by Becoming a Student* (New York: Penguin Press, 2006).

135   *"declining or stagnant"* Jay Shambaugh and Ryan Nunn, "Why Wages Aren't Growing in America," *Harvard Business Review*, October 24, 2017, https://hbr.org/2017/10/why-wages-arent-growing-in-america.

135   *income disparity* The Census Bureau uses four different summary measures of income disparity: the Gini index of income inequality, the mean logarithmic deviation of income (MLD), the Theil index, and the Atkinson index. "The Gini index is a statistical measure of income inequality ranging from 0 to 1, with a measure of 1 indicating perfect inequality (one household having all the income and the rest having none) and a measure of 0 indicating perfect equality (all households having an equal share of income). The Theil index and the MLD are similar to the Gini index in that they are single statistics that summarize the dispersion of income across the entire income distribution. The Atkinson measures are useful in determining which end of the income distribution contributed most to inequality." U.S. Census Bureau, "Income Inequality Metrics," https://www.census.gov/topics/income-poverty/income-inequality/about/metrics.html (accessed April 20, 2019).

135   *the lowest economic fifth* Household income disparity in 1977 and in 2017 is based on the author's calculations using data from the U.S. Census Bureau. Kayla Fontenot, Jessica Semega, and Melissa Kollar, *Income*

and Poverty in the United States (Washington, D.C.: U.S. Census Bureau, 2018), 35–39, https://www.census.gov/library/publications/2018/demo/p60-263.html. The jump in income data from 1977 to 2017 of economic quintiles was calculated by the author from these same charts.

136 *Race and gender* Fontenot, Semega, and Kollar, *Income and Poverty in the United States*, 6, 9. Also see in the same source figure 1, "Real Median Income by Race and Hispanic Origin: 1967–2017," 5; and figure 2, "Female-to-Male Earnings Ratio and Median Earnings of Full-Time, Year-Round Workers 15 Years and Older by Sex: 1960 to 2017," 9.

136 *more likely to be living in poverty* For poverty rates by race and gender, see Fontenot, Semega, and Kollar, *Income and Poverty in the United States*, table 3, "People in Poverty by Selected Characteristics: 2016 and 2017," 12.

136 *"squeezed by both declining incomes"* Jenny Schuetz, "Is the Rent 'Too Damn High'? Or Are Incomes Too Low?," Brookings Institute, December 19, 2017, https://www.brookings.edu/blog/the-avenue/2017/12/19/is-the-rent-too-damn-high-or-are-incomes-too-low/.   Schuetz   also argues that the plight of low-income families is not simply a result of the recession. She explains: "In 2015 the median renter in the bottom quintile of the income distribution spent 11 percentage points more of their income on rent than they did 15 years earlier in 2000 . . . This increase in rent burdens occurred through each business cycle period including the period prior to the financial crisis (2000–2006), the economic downturn (2006–2009), and the subsequent recovery (2009–2015)." To see original report from which these statistics are drawn, refer to the next note.

137 *56 percent of total income* Jeff Larrimore and Jenny Schuetz, *Assessing the Severity of Rent Burden on Low-Income Families* (Washington, D.C.: Board of Governors of the Federal Reserve System, 2017), https://doi.org/10.17016/2380-7172.2111.

137 *Pulitzer Prize–winning book* To read about the plight of families facing eviction, see Matthew Desmond, *Evicted: Poverty and Profit in the American City* (New York: Crown Publishers, 2016).

137 *"Severe" housing problems Worst Case Housing Needs: 2017 Report to Congress* (Washington, D.C.: U.S. Department of Housing and Urban Development, 2017), iii, https://www.huduser.gov/portal/sites/default/files/pdf/Worst-Case-Housing-Needs.pdf.

137 *high-income renters America's Rental Housing: Expanding Options for Diverse and Growing Demand* (Cambridge: Joint Center for Housing Studies of Harvard University, 2015), 3, http://www.jchs.harvard.edu/research-areas/reports/americas-rental-housing-expanding-options-diverse-and-growing-demand.

138 *"Fewer than one in four eligible families"* Schuetz, "Is the Rent 'Too Damn High'?"

139   *"high cost of being poor"* Sandra L. Barnes, *The Cost of Being Poor: A Comparative Study of Life in Poor Urban Neighborhoods in Gary, Indiana* (Albany: State University of New York Press, 2005).

140   *6.5 percent of all U.S. households* These are estimates from 2017. Another 18.7 percent of U.S households are considered "underbanked," meaning that they may have a bank account but regularly use services other than a bank to pay bills and borrow money. *2017 FDIC National Survey of Unbanked and Underbanked Households* (Washington, D.C.: Federal Deposit Insurance Corporation, 2018), 1, https://www.fdic.gov/householdsurvey/2017/2017report.pdf.

Survey data on unbanked and underbanked households and their use of financial services can be found at "2017 FDIC National Survey of Unbanked and Underbanked Households," Federal Deposit Insurance Corporation, https://www.fdic.gov/householdsurvey/ or "2017 FDIC National Survey of Unbanked and Underbanked Households," Federal Deposit Insurance Corporation, https://economicinclusion.gov/.

140   *"Do not have enough money"* In 2015, 57.4 percent of unbanked households cited this as a reason. For more information, see *2015 FDIC National Survey of Unbanked and Underbanked Households* (Washington, D.C.: Federal Deposit Insurance Corporation, 2015), 3, https://www.fdic.gov/householdsurvey/2015/2015report.pdf.

141   *"non-bank credit"* *2015 FDIC National Survey of Unbanked and Underbanked Households,* 9.

141   *40 percent of unbanked* "Pawn Industry Statistics," National Pawnbrokers Association, 2016, https://assets.nationalpawnbrokers.org/2016/05/PawnFacts.pdf.

141   *A full 80 percent* "Pawnbrokers Report Decrease in Retail Sales as Online Competition Grows and Buying Trends Shift," National Pawnbrokers Association, 2017, https://www.nationalpawnbrokers.org/2017/pawnbrokers-report-decrease-in-retail-sales-as-online-competition-grows-and-buying-trends-shift/.

142   *TITLE LOANS ARE EXPENSIVE* "Car Title Loans," Federal Trade Commission, last modified July 2014, https://www.consumer.ftc.gov/articles/0514-car-title-loans.

142   *one in eight pays the loan off Single-Payment Vehicle Title Lending* (Washington, D.C.: Consumer Financial Protection Bureau, 2016), 4–23, https://files.consumerfinance.gov/f/documents/201605_cfpb_single-payment-vehicle-title-lending.pdf.

143   *"Loans typically cost 400%"* "How Payday Loans Work," Consumer Federation of America, http://www.paydayloaninfo.org/facts (accessed April 20, 2019).

143   *36 percent of his or her next paycheck* "Payday Loan Facts and the CFPB's Impact," Pew Charitable Trusts, January 14, 2016, https://www. pewtrusts.org/en/research-and-analysis/fact-sheets/2016/01/payday-loan-facts-and-the-cfpbs-impact.

143   *more payday loan lenders* The media are fond of reporting this, and references to McDonald's, Starbucks, or both have appeared in this context on CNBC News (November 24, 2014) and in the *New York Times* (October 4, 2017), the *Washington Post* (May 26, 2014; June 27, 2016), *Business Insider* (Jan 30, 2017), and *The Atlantic* (May 2016).

143   *two-thirds of the total revenues* Payday loans offered by the industry are estimated to account for 66.7 percent of total industry revenue according to the Consumer Federation of America's Payday Loan Consumer Information website, https://paydayloaninfo.org/.

143   *more than ten thousand pawnshops* "Pawn Industry Statistics," National Pawnbrokers Association, 2018, https://nationalpawnbrokers.org/ assets/2018/02/FAQ_2018.pdf.

143   *"we're always adding new ones"* The auto title loan website and statistics can be found at "List of Companies That Offer Online Title Loans," Car Title Loan Lenders, last modified April 10, 2019, http://www. cartitleloanlenders.com/list-of-car-title-loan-lenders/.

143   *AF$PA* Alternative Financial Service Providers Association, accessed April 20, 2019, http://paydaybrokers.com/.

143   *"industry's leading voice"* The FiSCA website and its lobbying platform can be found at "Welcome to FISCA," Financial Service Centers of America, https://www.fisca.org/ (accessed April 20, 2019).

144   *also maintain PACs* The National Pawnbrokers Association maintains its own political action committee, which it presents this way to its members: "In today's political environment, voting is not enough to ensure your voice will be heard. There is [sic] thousands of special interest groups involved in politics, all of them competing to have their ideas accepted by lawmakers. Voting may help you elect the right people, but by itself it's no guarantee they know our business or understand the impact legislation will have on us. This is where the NPA PAC can make a difference. Your PAC contributions give us the edge in competition and ensure lawmakers know who we are as an industry." "Government Relations," National Pawnbrokers Association, https:// www.nationalpawnbrokers.org/government-relations/ (accessed April 20, 2019).

144   *the first two threats* "Check Cashing & Payday Loan Services Industry in the US," IBISWorld, August 2018, https://www.ibisworld.com/industry-trends/specialized-market-research-reports/advisory-financial-services/ intermediaries/check-cashing-payday-loan-services.html.   IBISWorld is a global business intelligence leader specializing in industry market

research. Its reports are proprietary, accessed for a fee, but part of each
report is public.

144   *Military Lending Act* The act, which was passed on July 21, 2015, also
applied to active duty National Guard and Reserve forces. See https://
www.fdic.gov/regulations/compliance/manual/5/v-13.1.pdf.

144   *regulate the payday loan industry* A factsheet summarizing the CFPB rule
on payday loans is available at https://files.consumerfinance.gov/f/docu-
ments/201710_cfpb_fact-sheet_payday-loans.pdf. The full CFPB rule
on payday loans is available at https://files.consumerfinance.gov/f/docu-
ments/201710_cfpb_final-rule_payday-loans-rule.pdf.

144   *"a right to financial freedom"* Eric Norrington, "Chairman's Message,"
Financial Service Centers of America, https://www.fisca.org/FISCA/
Content/Chairman-Message.aspx?hkey=0fc88f49-38d9-4561-97ac-
84d9a5b01ad9. (accessed April 20, 2019).

145   *"crippled the new rule"* The *New York Times* reported on February 6, 2019
that, under CFPB bureau director Kathleen Kraninger, "Payday lenders
won a major victory on Wednesday after the Consumer Financial Protection Bureau moved to gut tougher restrictions that were to take effect
later this year." Stacy Cowley, "Consumer Protection Bureau Cripples
New Rules for Payday Loans," *New York Times*, February 6, 2019, https://
www.nytimes.com/2019/02/06/business/payday-loans-rules-cfpb.html.
   The CFPB website quote can be found at: "Payday Loan Protections,"
Consumer Financial Protections Bureau, https://www.consumerfinance.
gov/payday-rule/ (accessed July 23, 2019).

146   *"NIMBYism"* The work done here on "not in my backyard" (NIMBY)
issues dates from March 2010, during the Obama era. To find it, you
must be persistent if you are just clicking through the current HUD
Exchange government site because the "Homeless Prevention and
Assistance" tab is no longer featured. Find it in the Resource Library at
"Nimby Assessment," HUD Exchange, https://www.hudexchange.info/
resources/nimbyassessment/?nimbyassessmentaction=main.dspnimby-
overview (accessed September 10, 2018).

146   *"vandalizing building sites"* "NIMBY Assessment: Identifying NIMBY
Attitudes," HUD Exchange, https://www.hudexchange.info/resources/nim
byassessment/?nimbyassessmentaction=main.dspnimbyattitudes (accessed
September 10, 2018).

147   *National Alliance to End Homelessness* The National Alliance to End
Homelessness's website address is https://endhomelessness.org/, where it
provides rich resources including demographics on homelessness, pub-
lications and toolkits on homeless issues and advocacy, and suggestions
for community action. The organization advocates for a community-
wide approach—rather than a response of individual agencies—where a

variety of coordinated approaches, such as rapid re-housing, supportive housing for the vulnerable, crisis response, and increasing employment and income are employed. See https://endhomelessness.org/ending-homelessness/solutions/ for the group's latest suggestions for community solutions.

For specific populations of homeless people or special issues, there are additional useful sites, including for homeless veterans (National Coalition for Homeless Veterans, http://www.nchv.org/), for homeless children (Stand Up for Kids, http://www.standupforkids.org/), for legal issues and advocacy (National Law Center on Homelessness and Poverty, https://nlchp.org/), and for policy and training involving health care for the homeless (National Health Care for the Homeless Council, https://www.nhchc.org).

147   *Gross National Happiness* Bhutan's official Gross National Happiness website can be found at http://www.grossnationalhappiness.com/. The website contains selected articles about the nine pillars and about how the index is constructed and used. The website explains: "The GNH index supports policy-making within Bhutan. Policy selection tools are used to review the potential effects of proposed policies on GNH and the results of the GNH index will be tracked over time to evaluate interventions."

149   *Which error* Of course, there are alternatives when encountering a panhandler who is clearly inebriated or compromised, when a cash gift seems unwise: an offer of food, a bus pass, a pair of clean socks, or a kind word.

151   *caution and critical judgment* Jason worked long enough at a shelter to know that, as with anywhere else, there are pitfalls to dropping your guard indiscriminately. He recalls one time when he was physically attacked by a client. Ross has shared, *"I mean I've been there. I know when people feel their backs up against the wall what they're capable of."* There are some homeless people—particularly those with addictions—around whom Cathy has felt unsafe, and many situations in which she guards her personal information.

Index

About the Authors

Cathy A. Small is professor emerita of anthropology at Northern Arizona University and a resident of Flagstaff, Arizona, where she enjoys life with Phyllis, her spouse of thirty years. A dedicated practitioner and teacher of Buddhist meditation, she offers talks, classes, and retreats to community members and inmates at the county jail.

Jason Kordosky is a researcher for the Culinary Union, where he helps workers fight for fair wages, job security, health insurance, pensions, and safe working conditions. He works and lives in Las Vegas, Nevada, with his spouse, Magally, and his best cat friend, Tobie. He enjoys hiking, photography, and writing poetry in his free time.

Ross Moore is a proud disabled Vietnam veteran and resident of northern Arizona. After surviving three decades of recurrent homelessness, he now lives with his wife, "Wendi," in a HUD-subsidized apartment. His citizen rights have been restored after he lost them in his twenties following felony convictions for burglary. He is an avid collector of vinyl records.